# 1.3 BILLION

# 1.3 BILLION

## A FOOTBALLING REVOLUTION IN THE MAKING

## SHIV JHANGIANI

NEW DEGREE PRESS

1.3 BILLION

*A Footballing Revolution in the Making*

ISBN   978-1-5445-0024-9  *Paperback*
       978-1-5445-0025-6  *Ebook*

# CONTENTS

# ABOUT THE AUTHOR

Shiv Jhangiani is the founder of Billion Dollar Foot, a sports advisory firm helping clubs, organizations and brands build connections to India and its football. Shiv is a former aspiring professional footballer and currently an entrepreneur. Serious knee injuries knocked his promising youth football career off track but that didn't deter his passion for football and his homeland.

Shiv has lived in seven different countries developing an undeniable passion for traveling and discovering new cultures. Ever since moving to Nigeria at the age of two the one thing that Shiv would never leave his sight is his football. From Nigeria to DC, via London, Atlanta, Vienna, Athens, New Delhi and Metz, he has been head-over-heels for the 'beautiful game'. Shiv spent three years playing for FC Metz's youth teams, an academy that has spat out the likes of Robert Pires and Miralem Pjanic amongst other legends of the game. Unfortunately, for Shiv his dreams came to an abrupt halt when he tore his ACL twice and menisci four times in the space of twenty months.

Shiv connected his passion for football and India to delve into the business of Indian football during his time at Georgetown University. He plans to be on the pitch in some shape or form when the World Cup finals are hosted in India in the (very) near future.

# ACKNOWLEDGEMENTS

Ask anyone that knows me and they will tell you that I'm probably the last person they would have expected to write a book... But, what they would tell you is that football is more than just a part of my life. Whether I'm planning my weekend around Premier League kick off times or spending my summers following World Cups and European Championships; it has always been all about football. Getting to this stage would have never been possible without a lot of people that have supported me on the way and I need to thank each and everyone of them. Firstly, my parents and my sister for always supporting me and pushing me further, and further. To some of my closest friends who got me back on track and made me stick it out till the end. To everyone that I held interviews with to gather the information and the stories I needed to put this together, your time and help has been priceless to me.

Finally, to Eric Koester for guiding me through the process step-by-step, without your help and advice I'm not sure I would be sitting here today with the final product I have.

# PROLOGUE

---

*"I don't know where home is."*

*"Yeah you do. It's green and it's got a goalpost at each end."*

I don't think I've ever been able to relate more to a line from a movie. Ever since I can remember the easiest question to answer for me has been, "what do you want to be when you grow up?". Not, "where are you from?" or "where's home?". Apart from family, the one mainstay throughout my whole life has been football. It has been one of the only things that stayed true to me through all the changes in my life, and one of the only things that I swore to always stay true to. Where most kids would have stuffed toys on their bed, I would have footballs. Where most kids would watch cartoons, I would watch football. Where most kids would play with Lego, I would play with a football.

Not seeing someone fly my country's flag in the entire world of football doesn't just bother me though, it kills me. I had always dreamt of being the one to start a movement and put India on the map in footballing terms.

This book is my way of showing the world of football what it is missing out on in the shape of India. I'm still only 19 but just haven't figured out what I want to do in life yet. Everything I did was building up to me being a footballer and making that my whole life. Things didn't quite work out down that road but now I am focused on finding a path back into the world of football, and specifically into the business of the beautiful game — and bringing it to my native India would just be the icing on the cake.

# INTRODUCTION

---

"Some people think football is a matter of life and death. I don't like that attitude. I can assure them it is much more serious than that."

"I eat, I sleep, I breathe football."

## 23RD OF JUNE 2013: METZ, FRANCE

The last day of the season, my first season at FC Metz's 'centre de formation'. I was lined up with my teammates, ready to play our last game of the year before we all went home for the summer. The blazing sun made it hard for me to believe that I was in the same city that in February punished me to 3 weeks of -15 degrees Celsius. The heat rising through the astroturf and my shoes burning the soles of my feet. Singapore's U18 national team were our opponents and they were captained by, my then best friend, Adam Swandi - one of the country's most promising athletes. Coached by Christophe Walter, ex FC Metz and Stade de Reims player, we were set up in a 4-2-3-1.

I was in my element. I showed up to the game with the perfect balance of cool and butterflies in my stomach. I walked into the locker room in my flip flops, headphones on, music blasting and my football boots in hand. I was in the zone. Puling my socks on, I was concentrated and relaxed. The warm up was nothing out of the ordinary, your classic ten-metre jogs, sprints, long balls and small sided games. Little nutmegs and flicks around the corner... I could just tell I was getting in the mood. It had been a while since I remember feeling so good and confident on the pitch. Everything I tried came off, even the Paul Scholes-esque cross field long balls off my piece of shit left foot were finding their targets! I was zig-zagging my way through the opponents, ordering everyone around and just bossing it from the back. From stepping up for offside traps to whipping crosses into the corridor of confusion, I was having an absolute fucking field day.

I remember the half time whistle going and I jogged over to the bench with the most obnoxious and arrogant look on my face. After going through a year of being one of the worst players on the pitch day-in-day-out it was an amazing feeling to get back into the swing of things. Before getting to France I coasted through every single game and training session I had been through in my life. Coming to Metz hit my confidence like a mother fucker. I had gone from being a big fish in a small pond, to a small fish in the ocean. I was scared to try things, scared to shout, scared to shoot. I just didn't feel natural and wasn't playing to my instincts. Playing football used to be like riding a bike, I wouldn't have to think before doing anything but now it was different. Now I was overthinking everything. It wasn't that I was one of the worst players there, it was that I needed to adapt. Adapt to a new place, a new team, a new culture, but most importantly a new football. I wasn't used to playing at such a high intensity, where every challenge was do or die. A style of football where every millimetre was key. My confidence started picking up around halfway through the season and good performances were definitely boosters. It was tough adapting to France. I had moved around a lot, living in 6 different countries already. The big difference, though, was that everywhere I went, everyone was used to travelling and moving around. I was in the biggest international school in the biggest city of each country. And then butt-fuck-middle-of-nowhere Metz came along. I gave up my whole social life, to move to the tiny French town in pursuit of my dream. I came in as a complete outsider, not speaking the language and not sure of what to expect. It took me a while to settle in and adapt. After a few months though, I was starting to fit in and belong. I began earning respect on and off the field when my efforts started to show.

Going back to the game; that day felt different - it felt like being back at home. Being back at the top of the game, being back to playing football the way I knew how to. The only difference was that this time, I actually deserved to feel like that because I was playing for one of the best youth teams in the world. Without a doubt the most intuitive 45 minutes of football I had played in my life. Everything I did just felt right, I was starting to feel at home on the pitch again. I just knew what was right and when it needed to be done. I just played it simple. It's exactly what Johan Cruyff said, "Playing football is very simple, but playing simple football is the hardest thing there is." Cruyff is arguably one of the most innovative men in football, and what he said didn't seem too bloody complicated to me today.

I walked back onto the pitch, really just feeling comfortable and at home - for one of the first times in my whole debut season at Metz. The first 20 to 30 odd minutes of the second half were a continuation of everything from the first half. 72 minutes into the match, Singapore's holding midfielder played a looping ball over the top of my head for his left winger to run onto. I followed the ball in the air, blocking out the sun with one hand, while turning into position at right back. I took a glimpse over my shoulder, whilst running back towards my own goal, to see if anyone was on the chase. It looked like their number 6 had over hit the ball and that it was going out for a throw, but I continued to shepherd it out just in case. Just as the ball had crossed the line to go out of play, I turned to see the Singaporean left winger launch himself at me. Studs first, flying through the air as I pivoted with my right leg rooted to the ground, he battered into my upper calf. I heard a snap and then didn't remember the next few minutes.

That feeling of blacking out that is associated, almost always (admittedly in my case as well), with having a few too many drinks is what I had. The excruciating pain just wiped my memory of the moment. All I remember is collapsing to the ground and grabbing hold of my right knee with my right arm, whilst covering my face with my left. The next thing I remember is the sight of my knee - a fucking train wreck. It was four to five times its size, battered and bruised. Completely swollen and covered in ice. I struggled to move my toes. Thus far, I had experienced my fair few ankle twists and the odd (three to be precise) broken collar bone, but nothing too serious (at least that's what a sports doctor convinced both my mother and me).

*I remember the process of going through a medical with a doctor, and my mother.*

*"Any injuries?" he asked. I looked over to my mum, gesturing for her to answer as any normal 14-year-old would. And just as any other over-protective mother would, she obliged with a "way too many, Doctor! Let me give you the whole list!" After a*

*few minutes of my mother reciting every single thing she could think of, from cuts to bruises to broken bones, several of which I still think she made up to exaggerate, the doctor silenced her. "Wow… That's it? You should count yourself lucky!" I remember grinning at the blank and, quite bluntly, stupid look on my mum's face.*

This time, however, I had a feeling it was something serious. I just had a feeling and remember the snapping sound so well. The club's youth physio; however, was adamant (after barely examining my knee for a minute) that it was no more than a slight sprain. His justification of "I've torn every single ligament in my knee, trust me… If there was something torn, I would know," did not reassure me one bit. I know it sounds terribly cliché but I just knew. I knew that I heard a snap and this guy didn't seem to want to listen to a word I had to say (looking back now though, I don't know how keen I would have been to listen to a little Indian kid absolutely butcher the French language while attempting to describe the pain he felt in his knee just a day before jetting off to the South of France for the summer). So, I just gave up on him and as anyone nowadays does, I decided that self-diagnosing myself with the help of the internet was my best shot at figuring out what had happened to my knee. With the help of everyone who answered the *"My knee popped and hurts… HELP?"* question on Yahoo! Answers, I had come to find that the solution was quite simple really, *"lie on your back on floor with hands, palms down under bottom, and lift your legs and do peddling motion as if you are on a bike, slowly forward a bit and then peddle backwards. Usually it will pop right back in place,"* according to ILouise at least! Unfortunately, (but fortunately for the thousands of knee surgeons out there and their dependents), this extensively well thought out proposition didn't have its desired effect. Two weeks later, I got back to London but my mum wouldn't let me step foot at home before seeing a doctor. Sure enough, an MRI revealed that I had torn my anterior cruciate ligament (ACL) along with my medial meniscus. If I wanted to return to playing high intensity sports I was going to have to undergo surgery before going through a 6 to 8-month rehabilitation process.

I have lived a very good, very privileged life. But, a life with a lot of change and up until this point the only thing that had stayed constant for me was my love for football. Ever since the age of two I have never let my first world cup mini football leave my sight. It was a lot more than just a ball to me. It was an identity, a dream, and a safety blanket. It was the one thing that defined who I was, where I came from and who I wanted to become. Through seven countries, eight cities, and six languages, my football was my only remaining sense of home.

But, now even football was gone. *Fucking hell.* That was the only thing going through my mind. At first, I was just in a state of shock. It was as if I had just lost a family member. I didn't want to see anyone or talk to anyone.

That was without a doubt the one and only moment in my life that I have ever questioned my love for football (and even then this was done with a ball at my feet and a Manchester United kit on). It just felt as if the one mainstay, the one aspect of my life that has always defined me, was about to screw me over too. Whether I was playing under the scorching sun on the tennis courts of Lagos or in the hailstorms of Luxembourg I had always given my heart and soul to the sport. Whether I was playing in the famous "grenat" (maroon in French) of FC Metz or I was just kicking a ball around in my towel after a shower, I had dedicated everything to football. It was all about the game. But, now the game was gone for almost a year.

Three major surgeries and seventeen months of intensive rehabilitation later, I have not lost an ounce of love for the beautiful game. Even though, I will never get back to playing the same way I used to; with the same ease and at the same level. As cheesy and stupid as it may sound, it was love at first kick. There is not a day in my life that will go by without me either watching or playing some football. From days I would be trekking in Rishikesh, or spending days at the Opera in Vienna or even from the hospital beds I was in recovering from surgery - football has been a part of every single day of my life and will continue to be. It is unparalleled to me. It is more than just a part of my life; it is my life.

Today, football is without a doubt the most global sport there is. Played in over 200 countries by people from all types of different backgrounds and skin colours. The culture of football though, and the role it plays, is unique to each and every country. The two regions of the world that have dominated the game historically, and continue to do so, are Europe and South America. Out of the 20 World Cup tournaments there have been, only eight different nations have won it and each one of these nations is from either South America or Europe. The rivalry between the two regions is undeniable, European countries currently lead the way in terms of World Cups won (11 compared to 9 for South American countries).

On the club football front; however, there is no discussion to be had. The epitome of club football, and even football more generally in many peoples' eyes, is the Champions League. European clubs have the best reputation and attract the best talent in the world. Globally, the European football scene is relatively similar given that the majority of talent is European but there is a strong South American presence in the English and Spanish leagues. The prominence of African players in the French league and, to a much lesser degree, the English league is undeniable. Over two thirds of players in the Premier League are foreign with 6 continents and over 60 countries represented. Football has reached virtually every country in the world and my favourite statistic is that there are more nation members in FIFA than there are in the UN.

While every continent (bar Antarctica) is represented in the big 5 European leagues (England, Spain, Germany, Italy, France) the *crème de la crème* of the game has always been either South American or European. The Ballon d'Or is the supreme individual prize in football - it is awarded to the best player in world football. Ever since 1995, the year in which the rules were changed to allow non-Europeans to win the award, there has only been one winner outside of Europe and South America. George Weah of Liberia won the the award in the first year that the rules were changed, but since then there has not even been a single non-European/non-South American amongst the three final nominees for the award. The dominance of the game has been held for a long time by these two continents, but this does not discount from the fact that football is truly a world sport.

However, one of the very few countries in the world that football seems to have 'missed' is my home country, India. You would think after nearly 100 years (or 200 depending on your take on the history of the British Empire in India) of dominance and leaving the country in a state of civil war, the least the Brits could have done is give us the gift of football. But, no. A country with just over 1.3 billion people "cannot seem to put together a team of 11 guys who can kick a ball" in the wise words of Russell Peters. It, quite obviously, is not as simple as I might make it sound but, I for one find it mind boggling that there is yet to be an Indian player to have made an appearance for a club in the top 5 leagues in Europe. One thing we Indians are good at though, is criticising each other and making excuses so we're pretty okay with it generally speaking. There has been a concerted effort to promote the game more and more in recent years with the likes of Leo Messi and Bayern Munich having graced India with their presences. However, there is yet to be that big breakthrough launching Indian football onto the world scene.

I don't believe that there is no footballing talent to be found in India, in fact, I think it is quite the contrary. I am almost certain that India is a gold mine for footballing talent but the problem is finding and nurturing this talent. The question that needs to be asked is not, *is there talent in India?* but rather *if David Beckham was born in India, would he have ever kicked a football?* And, *would Messi have become the world star he is today if he were brought up in India?*

The questions I want to answer are:

Why football is crying out for India?

How does football need to be built in India?

How does the talent need to be found in India?

The first club, to have an Indian player will not only open the floodgates in football to India, but will also establish themselves as trailblazers, leaders, and specialists in the world of football.

# PART 1

# THE OPPORTUNITIES IN INDIAN FOOTBALL

Football is without a doubt the world's favourite sport. It is the most played and most watched sport in virtually every single country in the world. India, however, is not one of these countries. The sheer size of the country and the love for sport instilled in its people couple to give India the potential to be the next big talent pool in world football.

In the first part of this book, I will prove why football as a sport is crying out for India. The love for the sport in India is undeniable but it continues to live in the shadow of cricket and I will look at the changing landscape of sports in India.

The opportunities in Indian football are endless and given that the market is completely untapped and raw it makes it that much more attractive. The first club to sign an Indian player will have hundreds of thousands of players to pick from and, perhaps more importantly, will open themselves up to a market of 1.3 billion new people. The financial opportunities on offer in developing the sport in India and entering the market at ground zero are ones that should not be missed.

With a large number of European clubs beginning to plant seeds in India in hopes of unearthing Indian talent, the time is now to cease the opportunity whilst the home to the Taj Mahal is still an "unexploited and undiscovered territory in terms of football".

# CHAPTER 1

# WHY FOOTBALL IS CRYING OUT FOR INDIA

---

*"To wake up a sleeping giant you need more than one alarm clock. We have put different alarm clocks here. And I have to say the giant is not any longer sleeping, it's already starting to wake up,"*

SEPP BLATTER, EX-FIFA PRESIDENT, ON INDIAN FOOTBALL

Million Dollar Arm is a movie, based on a true story, about an American sports agent, JB Bernstein, who has been on a losing streak for as long as he can remember. Him and his partner were supposed to sign the "next big thing", NFL star, Popo. Popo ended up screwing JB and his partner over by signing for the big corporate sharks who offered him a million dollar signing bonus. They were pissed and went home.

Being Indian, JB's partner, Ash, naturally decided to turn on the cricket - just as any normal Indian would do at 3 in the morning when you're trying to get drunk and pass out... The two needed a win or they were going to go broke. During a discussion about their plans for the future, the pair realised that they needed to do something different; they needed to innovate and open the door to a new talent market.

JB: How about that baseball owner you know? What was his name?

Ash: William Chang. Big money guy out of San Francisco looking for investment opportunities in Asia. Except we don't have anything in Asia.

JB: Maybe we should find something. Think about Yao Ming. That dude's worth a hundred million in Chinese endorsements. We just need to find our Yao.

Ash: Okay. When it comes to China, we are late to the party. China's tapped.

JB: Fine, Taiwan.

Ash: Tapped.

JB: South Korea.

Ash: Tapped.

JB: North Korea.

Ash: Great. I'll set up a meeting.

JB: All right. Well, then, this. What if we go young?

Ash: Mmm-hmm.

JB: Find some kid, develop the talent. Get in on the ground floor.

Ash: Mmm. Hey, the Red Sox just signed an 8-year-old.

JB: All right. Maybe we hang out at maternity wards.

Ash: Yeah, last time I did that, I came home with twins.

What became clear in this conversation is that innovating in talent searches nowadays is one of the hardest things possible. Everything has been done. Literally everything. Baseball isn't even a globalised sport and these guys struggled to come up with an idea. Now imagine what this task would look like for a talent scout in football, unarguably the worlds most popular sport. To give you a quick overview of things, there are only 9 countries in the world with professional baseball leagues. The biggest stage in the sport is the MLB (Major League Baseball, and the American professional baseball league for those of you that are just as clueless about this sport as me). In the history of the MLB there have been 48 different nationalities represented. At the start of the 2015/2016 season the Premier League was home to players from 64 different countries. In just one season, more nationalities were represented in the English top flight than in the history of the MLB (despite there being 30 MLB franchises compared to 20 Premier League teams, and despite America being called the melting pot of the world).

Forget the MLB though. FIFA, the governing body of football worldwide, has more members than the United Nations. Just think about that.

"FIFA's mission is to develop football everywhere and for all, to touch the world through its inspiring tournaments and to build a better future through the power of the game."

The UN's mission on the other hand, "is to save succeeding generations from the scourge of war, which twice in our lifetime has brought untold sorrow to mankind, and to reaffirm faith in fundamental human rights, in the dignity and worth of the human person, in the equal rights of men and women and of nations large and small, and to establish conditions under which justice and respect for the obligations arising from treaties and other sources of international law can be maintained, and to promote social progress and better standards of life in larger freedom."

If you couldn't really be bothered to read that either, in a nutshell their mission is world peace. WORLD FUCKING PEACE. And FIFA, somehow, still has more members.

**Conclusion: the "new-world" play has been done. Unless, we discover extra-terrestrial activity sometime soon it looks like this play is done.**

Maybe there is another play though. Another strategy to could be used. "What if we go young? Find some kid, develop the talent. Get in on the ground floor." The problem, is that players are signing for clubs and signing contracts with clauses for future bonuses before they even turn 10 nowadays. You would think some of the European clubs had their scouts doing the rounds with the doctors in maternity wards looking for talent (honestly I wouldn't be too surprised if Arsene Wenger did though). All over Facebook and Instagram you see football fan pages posting game footage of 7 and 8-year-old kids advertising and marketing them, speaking about their upcoming trials… They barely started going to school and they're already having to go on trials to try and get into the best clubs in their regions.

**Conclusion: the age play has been done. Unless you can get a baby scoring a 30-yard screamer before they can walk, it looks like this play has been exhausted too.**

*The point of all of this, though is that IT IS NEAR-FUCKING IMPOSSIBLE* do something innovative in the search for talent in football. Almost every single one of the available options has been exhausted.

BUT, there is one option that springs to mind when thinking of innovation and emergence: a country... But, not just any country...

The second most populous country (and soon to be *most populous*, by 2022 according to the UN) and the fastest growing economy in the world. Home to one of the 7 'New' World Wonders and chicken curry. My home country and a lot, lot more...

**INDIA.**

*"You can't go wrong with a billion people. Because it's a developing country and it's, just now, starting to come into its own, financially, it is a huge untapped market"*

MARK CUBAN

With 5 out of 7 continents represented at the Round of 16 Stage in the last two World Cups, and FIFA having more nation members than the UN, the talent pool in football is well and truly globalised. But, India hasn't been hit yet. The sport of football has come to dominate the vast majority of our planet.

India, though, is a world apart; a world yet to be discovered, for the most part, by the beautiful game. Cricket is king in the Indian subcontinent but the ever-changing aspect of the game has led to the conclusion that it is not the most viewer friendly sport out there. Football on the other hand is, without a doubt, the most captivating sport there is. Football creates storylines that the likes of Spielberg and Scorcese could only dream of writing. Football will leave 9 year olds and 90 year olds alike with their hearts in their mouths. But, above all, football as a professional sport is very much unknown to a big part of India. With transfer fees rising well above $100 million for a single player, the beautiful game's market is escalating very quickly. There is a border-busting demand for players from all over the world and an injection of a new talent pool as big as India has to offer could very well be a big part in bringing things back to reality in the football transfer market. A new addition to the world of football would be more than welcome just about now. With almost every viable option exhausted thus far, India can provide football with the answer to its problems. There is new found hope in developing the game in India and with an upward trajectory, things really seem to be shaping up in India. The stage is set for the right investors to come in and take the sport to the next level in the subcontinent. The only question left is who will be the first to take the plunge and reap the rewards?

## CRICKET IS KING:

Football is a growing sport. It is estimated to be the second most popular sport in the country but a very, very distant second. The problem with that is that cricket takes the cake. To understand this, you must first understand that cricket is not just a sport in India. "Do you play cricket?" is not a question that you ask in India... What you need to ask is, "do you bat or bowl?". Sachin Tendulkar is one of the greatest players to have ever graced to sport of cricket, in India he is a God, and I don't mean that as an exaggeration. It really is a religion. Cricket has more influence in the country than politicians do! The only thing bigger than a Bollywood star in India is a cricket player.

The confusing thing, though, is that it makes absolutely no sense! The Brits invented cricket and it was supposed to be a sport reserved to the "aristocrats", sports like football and rugby are the ones for commoners. Yet, cricket is played by literally every child in India regardless of your background or caste. You see it being played in all surroundings, from the lushest of greens in New Delhi's scenic city-centre of Chanakyapuri to the streets of the slums. Cricket is the one thing that brings organisation to the most chaotic country in the world. The entire country came to a stand-still when we won the World Cup at the Wankhede Stadium in 2011. It takes a pretty special force to get the attention of over a billion people!

The positive about cricket is that it goes to show that sports are a part of the Indian identity and Indian values. Hockey is another other sport that has tended to attract attention in India, due to long spells of success at the international level. The point though is that sports plays a great role in India, and cricket occupies the same position in India that football does in England or Spain.

The story and development of cricket is a very interesting one. When cricket was invented, as I mentioned, it was supposed to be for the rich only, this is why cricket is known as "The Gentlemen's Game". The purest, most traditional form of cricket is a match that is played over five days in which each of the teams has two batting sessions and two bowling sessions, known as innings. Players are decked out in their "all whites" and the game goes on from morning till early evening, with breaks for lunch and tea. This was, initially, the way the game was meant to be played. Unfortunately, due to the monotonousness and lack of regular excitement, cricket failed to appeal to a wider range of spectators. In the 60's a new format of the game was introduced, which included shortening the length of the game to a single day and introducing coloured kits as well. This format is known as the ODI (One Day International). In 2003, the governing board of cricket continued in its vain of innovating and remodeling the sport by adding another format to the game: The Twenty20. Twenty20's basically pack into three hours, the same amount of excitement that used to be found in a Test (five day) match. Essentially, the Twenty20 is the shortest and sweetest version of cricket. The T20 is a marketable and spectator-friendly version of cricket - one that can attract a wider, more diversified audience than just cricket purists.

## FOOTBALL - STEPPING OUT OF THE SHADOW?

Apart from the format and the stop-start nature of the sport, one of the key differences between cricket and football is that the the calendar year in cricket revolves mostly around national teams. In modern football, on the other hand, the clubs tend to hold the bargaining power, for the most part at least (hence the outrage at the proposition of the 2022 World Cup in Qatar being moved to December).

If cricket can succeed and take the place it has in India despite the cultural differences between the identity of the country and the sport, there is no reason why football cannot. Firstly, football, at its core, has always been the sport for the "masses". It has been the sport that is open to every one. The sport that accepts rich and poor, black and white, girls and boys. In one of my favourite movies, Invictus, President Mandela and his squadron of cars roll down a road that separates on one side, a group of poor black children playing football and on the other, a group of white Afrikaners playing rugby. The rugby coach stops his boys to say, "remember this day boys, this is the day our country went to the dogs" whilst staring down the cars with the passing president and all the black children on the other side of the road. But, getting pack to the point - football is a sport that requires nothing but a ball to be played. That's what makes it accessible to everyone, everywhere in the world. Cricket requires a lot more material and organisation. While every single player is constantly involved in football and always moving, at least 9 of the 13 players on the pitch in cricket are typically inactive at any given time. Football is a lot more involving and accepting than any other sport.

Considering the fact that shortening the length of the game in cricket is what grew its audience and that the shortest cricket game still takes, on average, double the amount of time a football game does - does that not paint a picture? Football is a much more viewer-friendly sport.

The popularity of football has already picked up massively in India over the last few years. When scheduling games, European leagues look to cater to the Indian market as well and take time difference into account because of the financial opportunities involved in doing so, but I will come back to that later. Viewing figures for football in India are rising exponentially. Studies carried out by TAMSports show that football viewership in India between 2005 and 2009 rose by 60 percent. Audience reach for the World Cup in 2014 virtually doubled that of the same tournament in 2010 (44.9 million in

2010 compared to 85.7 million in 2014) according to a report by FIFA despite the awkward nocturnal timing of the games.

In spite of the growing popularity of the sport, there is still a lack of organisation at the professional level of football in India. India is one of the only countries in the world with different leagues that run in the same season with no links. The Indian Super League (ISL) is a club competition in India that was introduced in 2014. Before, there was only the I-League, which continues to be the only professional league in India that is recognised by the Asian Football Confederation (AFC). The ISL is a highly debated topic because many experts believe that its format does not help the development of football in India. Some have gone as far as to say that the ISL is "ruining the game". However, what the ISL has done is that it has proved to the world that there is an undeniable hunger for live, competitive football in India. In its first season, the ISL managed to muster up an average attendance of 24,357 which is only lower than those of the Bundesliga, La Liga and the Premier League. It is therefore the fourth biggest football league in the world in terms of attendances. Bigger than the French, Italian, Brazilian, Argentinian and Chinese leagues - countries in which football is a tradition that has been established for centuries and the one and only country in the world with a bigger population. Even though there is a blindingly obvious difference in quality between the ISL and the rest of these leagues, as well as the lack of connection to the teams, the ISL managed to outperform so many of the worlds best leagues in the world in terms of attendance in just its first season. Even in comparison with domestic cricket in India the ISL has been successful. The first of week of the 2014 season of the ISL had TV ratings of 170.6 million, the figures for this phase of the same year's IPL season was 184 million.

The success of the ISL in its first season, in terms of attendances and viewership figures at least, can be looked at as a "proof of concept" for a market for a football league in India. It silenced critics who claimed that football was nothing but a "sofa sport" where fans would sit at home to watch and debate foreign, mainly European, leagues without showing a real interest for Indian football. However, the ISL is still in the "potty training" phase. The early successes in viewership do prove that there is a market for a league in India, but a lot of modifications need to be made to the league for India to develop the sport properly and ensure that there is a platform in place for developing Indian talent to take off from. While developing a following and a fan base for football in India is without a doubt one of the most important steps, creating a structure for talent to emerge through is vital as well. There is definitely a wide fan base that is growing everyday in India and the talent is there to be found. All that is left is for the right investor to come in and exploit the market, before starting an avalanche of Indian footballing talent. The ISL has begun to put India on the map of world football, creating scope for Indian talent to be spotted. The new league has attracted attention to the Indian game and has provided opportunities for the talent in India to develop through grassroots programs as well as through playing with some of the biggest names in the game. With the attention and the nurturing of footballing talent in India, the stage is set for the first world class Indian player to be unearthed and turned into a superstar.

**TAKEAWAY:**

- Cricket might be king in India, but with over 1.3 billion people is there really only space for one sport?
  - In a word, no.
- While taking on cricket would just be outright insane, there is definitely a place for new sports in India.
  - The NBA has branded India as their next big target and it looks as though football is doing the same.
- With the demand for more football, both in terms of quantity and quality, all over the world there is a need for an injection of a new talent pool.
  - India is truly untapped and is exactly what coaches and CEOs at the biggest clubs in the world are looking for.
  - Potential for talent coupled with potential for profit make India the perfect new destination for football.
- The 2017 hosts of the Under 17 World Cup are underway to make themselves the next big thing in world football and there

could be no better time to take the plunge and dive head first into the Indian market.

## CHAPTER 2

# OPENING THE DOOR TO 1.3 BILLION

―――

*"India is resurgent. In 2015 its economy grew by 7.2 percent, faster than any other major nation. The travails of other emerging markets make this performance especially eye-catching: Russia and Brazil both shrank by more than 3 percent last year. Even China, long the world's growth leader, slipped behind India, growing at 6.9 percent. And in 2016 India is likely to hold its position at the top of the table. While China began January with a bout of confidence-sapping market turmoil, India is expected to grow at the same rate as last year—or possibly faster,"*

SEBASTIAN MALLABY, COUNCIL ON FOREIGN RELATIONS

India boasts of the fastest growing economy in the world as

well as the second biggest population. The government has made concerted efforts to bring more stability to the country and more transparency to its economy - the highly debated process of demonetisation is a great example of this. The hope is that these measures will attract more investors while allowing for space for development. The relentless growth of the Indian economy coupled with the increasing viewership and interest in the game of football, have set the stage for a footballing economy to be established in India. Despite the clear lack of structure and organisation that surrounds football in India, the potential is hard to deny. For the sport to develop at the professional level, the main challenge now is to get the avid football fans onto the pitch and creating players. While unearthing new talent is definitely one of the biggest opportunities in developing the sport of football in India, it is not the only one. India has a lot more to offer to football than just 1.3 billion potential new players or fans. Entering the Indian market will pave the way for an infinite amount of financial opportunities.

Let's get back to the guys from Million Dollar Arm for a second...

JB: I think I cracked this. They don't play baseball in India.

Mr. Chang: That's right. They don't. They play cricket.

JB: But we think that we can convert a cricket bowler into a baseball pitcher... Look, India is the last great untapped market. We find new fans there for American baseball, the financial opportunities are endless... Mr. Chang, if we can deliver to Major League Baseball its first Indian ballplayer, that's *a billion new fans.* What do a billion new fans need? *A billion hats. A billion T shirts.*

Mr. Chang: And you want to set this up like it's a talent contest?

JB: Exactly... That will ensure maximum exposure of talent to press... See, once we go over there and find these guys, we bring them back here, we train them in LA, and then we get them signed with a professional franchise.

The Million Dollar Arm program was initially a mere marketing stint. Whether the players became successful or not was never going to be too important. The important part of the program was "maximum exposure". Doing something innovative, and changing the game would lead to new opportunities. JB and Ash were banking on bringing two young Indians and training them to be Major League Baseball pitchers but they weren't doing this out of the good of their heart. They are businessmen and their end goal was inevitably a pay day. The marketability of these players, would be unparalleled because it opened the door to a billion new fans. Baseball had no presence in India, and no one really knew about the sport (except for Amit of course for those of you who have seen the movie). Whichever franchise ended up signing the players, whether they were actually good enough to ever play a game or not, was practically guaranteed to sell a million hats and t-shirts. The benefits of this program, though, were two-fold and that is important to understand. Firstly, in the short term the franchise's goal in signing the Indian players would be to gain publicity, grow their fan base, and hopefully make some bank through selling merchandise in India. Secondly, though, in the long term India benefits as well, and maybe even more so than the franchise. Having two players in the MLB sets a precedent, it leads the other teams to think there is a new market they can infiltrate to try and sign players from while increasing, or in this case creating, a fan base for the sport back in India. Sports is an industry that is unique in a lot of different ways. One of which is the way trends are set. Sports is an industry full of followers. As soon as one team goes and does something out of the ordinary, something that isn't necessarily the traditional way of doing things, all the other teams will be breaking their neck to try and follow in their footsteps.

In case you were wondering, Rinku Singh and Dinesh Patel, the two Indian pitchers whose stories were told in Million Dollar Arm, have yet to taste success. The two were signed by the Orlando Pirates back in 2010. Patel never made it past the rookie stage and moved back to India just two seasons later.

Singh is still going at it, but has the odds stacked up against him and doesn't seem likely to make the majors anytime soon...

Let's get back to the big picture though... Today, India has one of the most attractive economies that the world has to offer, with unmatchable growth rates and an increasing sense of security in business. The country presents a new opportunity in the footballing world because it really is one of the very few markets that has been left untapped. Though several big football clubs have a presence in India through partnerships with Indian corporates, it is important to note that clubs are yet to invest their own money in the country. The programs are branded with their names but financed, almost completely by Indian companies. The European clubs allow Indian corporations to use their name in order to market the programs for a fee and this is the model that is currently in place. Many clubs are looking to change this and get more involved in India now having seen some very promising signs in the past couple of years. In speaking with the FC Barcelona vice-president, Carles Vilarrubi, he assured me that "India is definitely a target for FC Barcelona". The sheer size of the country coupled with the undoubted sporting culture that exists in the subcontinent leave no space for doubt in the Barcelona VP's eyes that India has a lot to offer his club and the sport. In his words there is a "race" on between the top clubs of the Premier League and those of La Liga to really introduce football to India. Football has started to develop but has yet to really reach the country as a whole and he feels as though the first club or league to truly bring the sport to the whole country will enjoy a lot of success in the future. Admittedly, the Premier League clubs hold an advantage because of the cultural ties between England and India and because of the fact that the league sells their own TV rights which allows them to adapt and tailor to the Asian market. However, in footballing terms, India is still very much an "unclaimed territory" with no single club or league having really left a stain big enough to mark the country as their territory yet.

The "Million Dollar Arm strategy" is one that many sports teams have used before and enjoyed lots of success with. Manchester United is a great example. They signed Ji-Sung Park for a measly $4.5 million in 2005, to use his image in East Asia. Football gained further popularity in South Korea, after the boom in 2002 when they were co-hosts of the World Cup. Park was a success story that Koreans could relate to and felt attached to. He had proved to his nation that making it to the top of football wasn't beyond them. A cult following for Manchester United went hand-in-hand with sustained development of football in Korea in the years to follow. While the relationship between Manchester United and the former South Korean international was symbiotic, attempts to recreate the success didn't fare too well. Chinese youth international, Dong Fangzhou and American Tim Howard, didn't enjoy as much on-pitch success as Ji-Sung Park but Manchester United still achieved their purpose in infiltrating the American and Chinese markets thus proving the ingenuity of the strategy.

While some clubs will inevitably try the above mentioned strategy, India has a lot more to offer than just its immense population. The three big opportunities I am going to present are merchandising, pre-season tours and academies. In my opinion, these are the three most viable options that combine benefits for India (in developing football) and the potential investors in European football (profit) aside from anything to do with developing talent.

**MERCHANDISING:**

First off is merchandising, undoubtedly one of the most obvious options. In 2012, Adidas estimated that the sportswear market in India was worth nearly $500 million and around half of that was made up in football merchandise. Based on viewership figures, the football fan base in India has more than doubled since 2012 meaning that the value of the sportswear market has without doubt grown as well. The best part about the merchandising option is that it is a market that is just as attractive to fringe viewers of football as it is to the loyalists of the game (a group that is a lot smaller in size) which expands the potential number of clients exponentially. Because of the lack of local football in India, football junkies in the country are forced to watch the English Premier League, La Liga and the Bundesliga predominantly, to get their fix of football. Inevitably, these fans grow fond of certain teams and develop particular affinities to select sides. The big international teams can take advantage of the absence of their domestic rivals, as all the indigenous leagues' teams have yet to come of age with their merchandising. Teams like Real Madrid, Liverpool and Barcelona have had time to build loyalty that transcend their geographical limits. Estimates say that tie-ups of certain top clubs in India make around $45 million in revenue over two years and this number was announced over five years ago, and has therefore grown as well. The classic all-white of Real Madrid and blood red of Manchester United can be spotted all over India from the busiest malls of Mumbai to the most remote villages in Bihar. This is what makes it such an attractive proposition for clubs to enter the Indian market and further develop their presence.

An example of how this has worked, is yet again the story of Manchester United, a club that quite evidently has been one of the most successful in tapping into its global fan base. It was estimated that 27 out of 40 million South Koreans in 2011 were Manchester United (a big part of this was down to Ji-Sung Park playing for the Red Devils). The demand for Manchester United shirts, scarves, and hats was insane and a massive marketing opportunity for the club.

While sportswear might represent the biggest opportunities in merchandising, clubs aren't limited to shirts, hats and scarves. In Korea, while Park played for Manchester United, over 1 million credit cards with Manchester United branding were issued, with a royalty being awarded to the English club for each one. In fact, clubs have already started to innovate and look beyond apparel and accessories in the Asian, and specifically Indian markets. Manchester United have opened up cafés and bars in India with their branding while Chelsea teamed up with Indian bank IndusInd to distribute credit cards with some branding on them.

While the strategies in place in Europe seem to be working a charm for most teams, it is important to remember the difference between India as a market and most others. In developed countries like South Korea or most European countries, it is reasonable and accepted to charge anywhere between $90 and $200 for a football top. In India though, while the upper and upper-middle class would be able to afford these, the vast majority of the population wouldn't be able to afford these prices. The Chennai franchise of the ISL, officially sold 200 kits in their first season, but there were over 12,000 people donning the South Indian clubs colours. The chunk of these were fake copies that were being sold outside the stadium for Rs.200 to Rs.300 (approximately $3 to $5), around 3% of the price of what an actual replica would go for at a Nike, Adidas or Puma retail store.

There are a couple different things to notice in this situation.

1.  Affordability is a real issue when it comes to the sportswear market in India. This problem exists in several African countries, whose economies are fairly similar to India's, as well. But, to rectify this clubs ask their manufacturers to make two different versions of each of their kits: an actual replica (like the ones being sold in countries with developed economies) but also a cheaper, and lower quality version of this that can sell for a fraction of the place without eating into their margins. Employing a low-cost strategy in tandem with everything that is already in place can only serve to profit the merchandising giants like Adidas and Nike.

2.  This problem doesn't take away from the fact that the sportswear market in India is massive and has even greater potential to grow. Given that the current target audience for clubs to sell merchandise to in India is mostly made up of the urban youth from fairly well-to-do families, the emergence of e-commerce in India will allow them to tap into this lucrative sector with even more ease. The success of global giants like Amazon upon their entry into the Indian market will help in boosting these sales too.

## PRE-SEASON TOURS AND EXHIBITION MATCHES:

Another opportunity for clubs to enter the Indian market as a business initiative is through pre-season tours and exhibition matches. Primarily, pre-season fixtures are played for the players to gain match fitness before the start of the season. Just like most other things nowadays though, this has been turned into a money-spinner by most clubs. Travelling for pre-season was an innovation introduced to sports quite a while ago… Initially, the goal of doing so was to expose players to conditions tougher than the ones they were going to have to spend their seasons in. Clubs would usually fly their teams out to locations with high-altitudes, high-heat, and/or high-humidity. The goal of doing so was to make the conditions back home seem easy. This idea has evolved now though into a marketing project basically. Clubs jet off all over the world with some of the craziest schedules. America, Australia and more recently the Far East have been popular destinations for the likes of Arsenal, Real Madrid and Chelsea. It is such a great opportunity because clubs get offered significant amounts of money to go do exactly what they would have been doing somewhere else in the world only with the exception of adding on a couple publicity events. The clubs also get to raise brand recognition, reaching out to their global fanbases. The host countries are always happy to have the big clubs because the brands that are associated with them see their value skyrocket. Clubs make their decisions on which countries to visit based on two factors: the size of the pay cheque and the size of the market. (Although there seems to be a concerted effort to include the quality of football on offer as well as conditions in the country into the decision. This has led to multiple big European teams playing in tournaments abroad, and clubs shying away from the regions that are affected by monsoons.) The sheer size of India puts it ahead of any other country in the world with the exception of China. As for the money, as long as there is enough money invested there is no reason why India couldn't play host to some of the big hitters in football. With big stadiums and high levels of interest for football, especially in regions like Goa, Kolkata and the north eastern states, spectator response levels will be as high as they would be in any other country with a strong footballing culture.

In the previous example of Park Ji-Sung, Manchester United spent their first pre-season with Park Ji-Sung onboard on a tour of Japan and South Korea. United knew that their newly signed gem would appeal to the masses, guarantee that their fan base was fully engaged and that their spending was efficiently utilised. Another example of this is when Manchester United signed Javier Hernandez from Chivas Guadalajara. The Mexican club were adamant on including a clause in the sale of their then-star player, which would lead to Manchester United playing a friendly match to inaugurate their new stadium. This deal was mutually beneficial, because it helped Chivas attract attention, and sell tickets for a game while it offered United a way to leverage their popularity in a country that is still more connected to the Spanish league.

The proof of concept for this option in India has already been a success. In 2011, Argentina and Venezuela played a friendly match in the football capital of India, Kolkata (which used to be known as Calcutta). The game took place in front of 120,000 fans at Salt Lake Stadium, one of the largest football stadiums in the world. It is second only to the Rungrado May Day Stadium in Pyongyang, North Korea but for obvious political reasons (and the fear of Kim Jong-Un killing my ass) I won't say too much more about the country that convinced its population that they won the World Cup in 2010. This exact game would have never attracted anywhere near the same amount of spectators in either Buenos Aires or Caracas, but the desperation levels for football of a decent quality and the prospect of seeing Lionel Messi, a footballing god, in the blood and flesh was enough to pack the stadium to the rafters. Bayern Munich's visit of New Delhi received a similar reaction and was also a very successful event.

Pre-season tours, though, can tend to be a bit of a problem. For example, before the 2016/2017 season, Manchester United spent some time in China. Incessant rain led to the pitches being adjudged to be in unplayable conditions and led to training sessions and matches being called off. Jose Mourinho, the manager of the club, was understandably aggravated by the situation and added that he didn't want the public relation obligations of the club to hamper their ability to prepare for a season of football. In all honesty though, I don't see clubs turning down fat pay-cheques for more quality football in the pre-season anytime soon. But, pre-season tours can be a pain and can be expensive for the host countries - this is why, sometimes, exhibition matches can be a better option.

Exhibition matches can be just as effective as full-fledged tours with the added bonus of convenience. While clubs may be hesitant to spend more than a few days in India during the off-season given the weather conditions, a one-off exhibition match like the season openers that take place in Spain, Germany, France and England could be a great option. In these games the reigning champion of the domestic cup competition faces the previous season's league champion. The French League's initiative to take this match abroad to Tunisia and Canada had great success and could be a very simple model to replicate. The Italian equivalent to the Community Shield, the Supercup (a game in which the previous season's League and Cup champions meet to crown the ultimate champion of a given season), has been played in front of packed crowds in China and Qatar for each of the last six years. China and Qatar are both countries that have shown great interest in developing the sport of football in their own backyards but I'll get back to those stories a bit later on. Some teams even play games abroad during the winter break. The break can range from 2 weeks to a month during the Christmas/New Year's period depending on the country and the goal of this is to give the players a rest. England is the only European country that doesn't offer its teams this break. The way modern football is changing however, the winter break might not even be a break anymore. Team's use this time to their advantage, as they have to keep their players fit why not combine this with even more money.

While this option is clearly one that can, and has worked before, there is a lot of money involved with no tangible benefits to the pure developmental side of the sport.

## ACADEMIES:

A joint venture in setting up an academy is another viable option for European clubs to enter the Indian market. This option would appeal more to a small but academy-wise club like Southampton, West Ham United or FC Metz as it presents a more viable option to enter the Indian market for clubs with less international exposure. Denis Schaeffer, the Director of the academy at FC Metz, would be the first to admit this. The merchandising avenue is not one that would prove to be very lucrative for a club of the size of FC Metz as they can't compete with the likes of Juventus, Arsenal and Chelsea because they just don't have the same global image. The academy route is very attractive to smaller clubs because it is a strategy that they have mastered and continue to master in order to compete both on and off the pitch. Financially speaking, these clubs cannot compete with the likes of a Manchester City or a Paris Saint Germain nowadays who have sheikhs as owners and can write out blank cheques on a daily basis. The gulf that exists between the financial capabilities of the clubs cannot be understated. Therefore, the smaller clubs have to rely on creating and forming their own talented players rather than picking off players from others. The success they have enjoyed is down to a system that has been put in place in their respective academies which leads to a number of world class players being churned out every year. Forming these talented players is what allows them to keep themselves alive in the changing landscape of modern football that has come to be dominated by money. There is a law in FIFA regulations that requires that the club at which a player spent his formative years must receive a percentage of any sell-on fee paid for the players. In simple terms, this means that not only does the club benefit from the amount they receive to sell a player to another club, but they continue to receive money for every move the player makes in their career. For example, Southampton are the team that formed Gareth Bale and they received £7 million for the sale of the player to Tottenham in 2007. Then, in 2013, Bale transferred from Tottenham to Spanish giants Real Madrid for a world-record fee of over £85 million - of which Southampton received a percentage. This concept has lead to clubs like Southampton and West Ham United being able to perform fairly consistency in the Premier League under financial constraints.

FC Metz has historically been a talent factory for European

football. Situated right by the north-eastern border of France, FC Metz has taken advantage of the lack of big clubs in their region. They dominate the "grande région" which includes the regions of Lorraine, Alsace and Champagne-Ardenne in France as well as parts of Germany, Luxembourg and Belgium. They have produced the likes of Robert Pires, Miralem Pjanic, Louis Saha, and Emmanuel Adebayor but, they haven't limited themselves to this part of the world. FC Metz set up an academy in Dakar, Senegal (called Génération Foot) with the goal of recreating their academy set up in Metz in hopes of nurturing talent in the West African country. The French club owns 49% of the Génération Foot, which is enough to make major decisions without having to bear the full financial responsibility. The greatest advantage of this all is that they can find and sign talent in countries like Senegal for a fraction of the price that they would pay for domestic talent given the lower cost of living and other aspects that come into play. Génération Foot acts as an independent club, taking part in the league in Senegal but in reality it is a feeder club for FC Metz. There is a hierarchy and system in place where the three most promising talents at the Senegalese club graduate from the program in Dakar to the academy in Metz once they turn 18 and are legally eligible, according to FIFA laws, to sign for a European club. They then integrate the youth formation set up in France in hopes of signing a professional contract in the following years.

The success of FC Metz's partnership with Génération Foot is therefore not measured by the position in which they finish in the Senegalese league, it is measured by the number of players that go on to sign professional contracts in Europe. This program has produced some of the biggest names in European football today and has proved to be a success story for the French minnows. Sadio Mane, Diafro Sakho and Kalidou Koulibaly (who all ply their trades at Liverpool, West Ham United and Napoli respectively) are all graduates of the affiliation between FC Metz and Génération Foot.

The hope is that this program continues to produce talent and with 4 players in the current professional set up at FC Metz having come through Génération Foot, there is no reason to believe that this won't continue.

Success in Senegal, has led to the French club very seriously weighing up their options in India and considering doing something similar in India. They have already dipped their toes into the Indian market with several different projects and are keen to maintain and develop relations with the football landscape in the country. The relationship is very positive and promises to offer a lot to both parties in the near future. While this would be a long-term project in India, given that the sport would need to gain some momentum before it can spit out any promising talents, it could still be a very interesting project. In the early stages things would have to be different - there would have to be more of a "soccer school" feel to things where players pay fees to join the academy. This will set up an additional revenue stream for clubs and will also allow them to expend on setting up clinics to develop the game amongst the less fortunate. No club is going to get involved in Indian football on the sole premise of developing the sport in India - there has to be something for them to gain. The talent they can gain is not yet tangible, offering profits along with the idea of reaching out to the masses is an attractive opportunity for the clubs. It is one that will help with the PR and the finances all whilst developing their image in India. What India needs from a club like FC Metz is their expertise and know-how in the field of setting up an academy with all the right structures and values. India offers them another way of making money as well as creating a global identity for themselves.

## TAKEAWAY:

- The scope for development is being keenly monitored by a large number of Europe's leading clubs and the first team to take the plunge and really go all out in India could reap the rewards in the not too distant future.
- The financial opportunities on offer really are endless, and can be adapted for different teams and different target sectors of the Indian population.
- While bigger clubs can look to merchandising and pre-season tours to make money through the Indian market, this is

only possible because they can rely on a global image that they already have.

- Smaller clubs though, can go down the academy route to really develop the game itself in India as well as an opportunity to create a new revenue stream.

# PART 2

# BUILDING THE BEAUTIFUL GAME IN INDIA

The state of Indian football 5 or 10 years ago was quite simply abysmal. The problem is that today, whilst some progress has been made, in the grand scheme of things not enough has changed. There just doesn't seem to be any definitive progress and there is no real vision for the sport to develop under. No unified measures have been put in place to help us advance and take the game to the next level.

In this part of the book I will look to evaluate where Indian football currently stands by looking at the state of the main leagues, what a typical calendar year in Indian football looks like and where the national team sits. Then, I will try to see how we can tailor football to India, play to their strengths, turn their weaknesses into strengths and create an identity for Indian football as a whole.

CHAPTER 3

# THE (NOT-SO) BEAUTIFUL GAME IN INDIA

---

*"Football is trash," shouts one young boy, no more than ten years old.*

*Indeed, none of the dozen or so youngsters has even heard of Barcelona, Liverpool or the Manchester clubs. There is not a flicker of recognition at the names Messi or Ronaldo.*

*What makes this all the more ominous for those championing football in India is that the kids are playing cricket on a piece of land barely a mile (kilometre) or two from the training ground of the local football club Pune FC, a team which plays in India's top league.*

- BBC, 2014

To give you an idea of where Indian football stands today, let's first go through a quick overview of what a typical calendar year in Indian football looks like.

First off, you've got the Indian Super League (ISL), a league with 8 teams where every one of the teams plays each other twice each (home and away) in the group phase and then the top four go through to the play-offs. The ISL runs from October to December. Then, you've got the Hero I-League which is India's main professional league (meaning it is the Indian top-flight league in the books of the Asian Football Confederation, just as the Premier League is to England in the books of UEFA) that has 10 teams and operates from January to May. The Hero I-League works on a system of promotion and relegation with the I-League Second Division. There is no real set time or format for the I-League Second Division, though. It started in November in 2015/2016 but started the following January for the 2016/2017 season. Each year the number of groups and size of groups tend to be different with the play-off structure remaining fairly similar.

Apart from these leagues you have the Federation Cup which starts at the end of the I-League season and includes only the eight teams from the Hero I-League. Additionally, every state in India is suppose to conduct a state league that can be organised at any point that is convenient for them. The length of these leagues can vary from 2 weeks to 4 months.

Basically, what this goes to show is that there is NO such thing as a typical calendar year in Indian football, no matter what the governing body will have you believe (the AIFF have finally made concrete plans to merge the ISL and I-League in 2018). There is just no organisation when it comes to the league system. Can you imagine what the teams have to go through to try and plan their seasons? The AIFF requires that players in both divisions of the I-League contract their players for a minimum of 10 months but give them no guarantee of even a 4 month league. Clubs go into pre season not knowing when their season is even going to start. AFC Fateh Hyderabad, an I-League Second Division side, began their pre season for the 2016/2017 season at the end of August because they were told that the league would start in November. They figured they would have to start recruiting players and beginning training fairly early to gear up for a competitive season in which they hoped to achieve promotion to the first division. A couple weeks down the line, not only were the told by the AIFF that the start date would be pushed back to January but also that the format of the league was going to be changed.

"What do you mean change the format?"

"They want to separate the teams into 3 groups of 4 and the top 2 in each will go to the play-offs. The first round of the league will go from January till February and there will be a break in March. Then, the national round will be from April till May."

"Are you fucking kidding me? They expect me to contract my whole squad and staff for 10 months but my season could only last one month?"

How can a football club function like this? The basic answer is it can't and it doesn't.


**THE I-LEAGUE:**

The I-League is meant to be India's main, and only (up until the introduction of the ISL in 2014), professional league but the word professional really just glorifies a product that is not too glorious. The lack of professionalism in the structure does not cease to amaze. The governing body of Indian football, the AIFF, run this league and in 2010 they signed a 15-year deal with IMG-Reliance which gave the group commercial rights to sponsorship, advertising, broadcasting, merchandising, video, franchising as well as the rights to create a new league.

Put simply, the All India Football Federation took all the power away from each and every one of the clubs that participated in their leagues. They took away any means of making money. As it is, owning a sports team is one of the hardest things to do because of the challenging economics from owning a team. The majority of owners of I-League teams are business houses that run teams as a corporate social responsibility (CSR) initiative more than anything else.

Typically, a football club's revenue can be broken down into three equal parts: **merchandising, TV rights and player transfers** (there are definitely other ways clubs make money but these are the three that make up the chunk of it).

Given the lack of structure and authority in the game in India, enforcing contracts is almost impossible. In the history of Indian football there have only ever been two official transfers. Even calling it a "transfer window" is comical. I spoke to a coach at AFC Fateh Hyderabad, an I-League Second Division side, about his top players. Pre season was underway but a couple of their players hadn't shown up for training even though they were still contracted to the club. Later, he found out that his players had decided to play for teams in their home state league during their time off. They had done so behind their coach's back because they weren't given permission to play. The way their coach found out was the best part.

Both players had changed their WhatsApp pictures to pictures of them wearing the kits of their home-state teams they were playing for. When asked about these photos they claimed they were just supporting their hometown teams despite showing up on the scoresheet in multiple matches. Fateh decided to take action, and were encouraged by the AIFF to take action. However the bureaucracy and red tape typical to any government run board in India has led to no progress being made in 6 months. The takeaway is you can take player transfers and it's associated revenues off the table. **One third of potential revenues: gone.**

IMG-Reliance's takeover took away merchandising rights from the individual clubs. The worst part is that the group has done nothing to sell any merchandise for any of the clubs ever since the deal meaning that none of the clubs have any real presence. **Two thirds of potential revenues: gone.**

Broadcasting rights were another part of the deal between the AIFF and IMG-Reliance. There has been no live telecast of I-League matches for over 5 years now. **All gone.**

None of the three revenue streams that most football clubs usually rely on are available to I-League clubs so how can you look at owning a team in the league as anything other than a corporate social responsibility? The only reason people buy sports teams anywhere in the world is either to raise their profile or because they have a real passion for a game. It has been proven that you cannot make money out of owning a football team, and if you are making money and pulling out the profits then your team will not be doing well at all and it is not a sustainable plan. But, owners of I-League teams pump money into the clubs knowing full and well that they will never see it again. They don't even get the benefit of raising their profiles because there is virtually no media presence around the I-League… It wasn't till a few years ago that they even had a website! The combination of non-existent marketing, branding and telecasting lead to the league being run in complete obscurity. This has led to the league as a whole, and the individual clubs, losing value because they have zero media presence.

The positive of the I-League though, is that it follows a traditional league format - something that India needs. However flawed and unstructured it might be, the I-League is a necessity because it is the only real league that India has right now. The lack of progress it has made is worrying but if the right amount of glamour, structure and professionalism can be brought to the existing entity this could spell success.

## THE YOUTH LEAGUES:

The I-League did not even require, or offer much of an incentive for, its teams to field youth sides in the Under-18 version of the league until a couple of years ago. The bar is set so low with the requirements that the youth league might as well not exist. Clubs need only provide transport and kits for their youth players, the majority just sign deals with a local school team to go and represent them. Clubs are barely incentivised to put much capital into their youth teams since they only a receive a very small stipend for doing so and the tournaments barely last a month. Most teams will just pick a school team or academy from their home city, pay for kits and transportation and call this their youth team. It is just too easy to bypass the system and this is seen as one of the most glaring oversights on behalf of the AIFF.

A complete revamp of this system is what is needed. Youth leagues are the key to developing the sport and need to be completely restructured. If clubs can create a constant stream of players to come in not only will it increase the level of the game, it will provide more opportunities in the world of sport for youngsters.

## THE STATE LEAGUES:

State leagues aren't too different to the youth leagues. There is just no use of them. Apart from the leagues in Goa, Kolkata and Mizoram there is just a clear lack of quality and effort put into these. There is no structure because each one of these leagues operate at different times and there is no national level to these.

No other country really has anything like this, so why does it exist in India? Doesn't it just complicate the sport for no apparent reason? The only argument possible is that it allows smaller teams to grow, but this only applies to the three states that I mentioned earlier because they are the only ones that run properly. These could serve as good examples of how to run and format a league, and they also show the hunger for a well-run league with a wider variety of teams. There has got to be some sort of system put in place. Some of the clubs from the Goa, Kolkata and Mizoram state leagues for example are better than some of the I-League clubs because they attract local talent that other teams can't. Completely getting rid of these teams might not be the best way to go about things. Creating a system in which the state teams can form a pipeline to a smaller number of teams that compete at the national level is what needs to be done.

### THE ISL:

Until 2014, there was no domestic football of any quality available to Indian football fans. This is what opened the door to the introduction of the Indian Super League. The idea behind the ISL was to get some of the biggest international players who were past their prime to pass down their skills and knowledge to a youthful domestic talent pool all whilst attracting large crowds and developing an understanding/ love for the game across India. The ISL tried to follow in suit of the MLS, J-League (Japan), and A-League (Australia) who all started their rise to fame in similar fashion. The ISL attracted some of the most elite names in India, from

Bollywood stars to cricket legends as owners and the likes of Robert Pires, Nicolas Anelka, Fredrik Ljungberg, Luis Garcia, David Trezeguet and Zico graced the league with their presence as players or managers. The fact that these players were fading, and no longer capable of playing to the best of their abilities wasn't really a problem because they brought so much more to the table than just their playing ability. Apart from the commercial value that each of them hold, these players were key in passing on their experience and knowledge to the Indian youth, attracting sponsorship money, and made the ISL an enticing prospect for football fans across India and the world. The glitz and glamour of the league is, arguably, what led to its undeniable success in raising the profile of the beautiful game in India. The primary goal of the ISL was to get the people of India talking about football and to make the kids dream of playing professional football. With attendance levels exceeding expectations and rivalling those of the top leagues in the world (fourth highest average attendance in its first season) you can put a big tick next to that (as far as the first season goes at least). With viewership figures strong enough to rival the IPL in the first couple of weeks, there is no doubt that the ISL achieved that as well.

However, many have criticised the league saying that it doesn't put football at the forefront. I would argue that this is a necessary evil though. In India for anything to make a name for itself it has to be a "tamasha" but not just any type, it has to be a good "tamasha". The word "tamasha" is one that every Indian knows, regardless of how fluent their Hindi is. There can be a number of meanings for the word depending on the context, and the different meanings usually contradict each other. In most cases, though, the word means "a dramatic show", while this would typically have a negative connotation anywhere else in the world, you will not find a population that loves unnecessary drama more than Indians. I mean why else would you spend 3 hours (and have an intermission) watching a movie that could easily have been cut into less than half that time?! What I am trying to say is that for anything to be successful in India you must cause a commotion, but this commotion has to be accompanied with excitement. You've really got to go above and beyond to put on a show to win over the crowds in India. The success of Bollywood movies is purely based on going over the top in every aspect of every movie. From synchronised dances in war scenes to slow motion hair flips whilst crossing a street, the essence of Bollywood - what has allowed the home of Indian movies to be so successful - is the extravagance of it all. From the cheerleaders to the grand opening, the ISL certainly did provide the crowds with copious amounts of entertainment. The ISL managed, in one year, to bring something to Indian football that the I-League had struggled to do since it came into existence in 1996 - **entertainment**.

Unfortunately though, three years down the line the ISL is

beginning to experience a downward slope. Attendance levels dropped significantly in the third season, the promise of grass-roots programs don't seem to have been kept and generally speaking the state of Indian football doesn't seem to have improved all that much. The drop in attendance levels doesn't seem to have as clear-cut an explanation as one might think however. A big part of this drop off is down to the fact that the Kolkata and Mumbai outfits moved to smaller stadiums effectively cutting their capacities to half of what it used to be for Kolkata and one fifth in Mumbai's case. Clubs like Delhi and Pune who struggled to draw large crowds in from the get-go felt the impact with numbers falling further. Another effect is the underperforming teams like Goa who struggled to maintain the high standards they set for themselves in the early seasons which has led to a drop off in attendances. But, at the same time other clubs have experienced spikes in numbers so it really isn't as clear cut a picture as one might hope.

In spite of all of this, it is undeniable that the ISL did start a movement. The ISL got people talking about football in India and started to get some attention from the outside too. "I remember being in Delhi during the ISL and you had rickshaw drivers talking about the ISL. Debating whether Alessandro Del Piero, was a has-been, whether he was worth the money, and whether he was going to score in the next game. It was really just surreal". This is what Saptarshi Ray, a journalist for the Guardian recalled of his time in India during the first edition of the ISL. The conversations that you hear in pubs up and down England or in cafés across France between old men over a pint are what the footballing culture is really about. These conversations are taken for granted, but they are what show just how important the game really is. It used to be, "will Sachin (Tendulkar) score a century against England?" or "will India beat Pakistan?" but the ISL has achieved something that India has never quite managed before, **it made football a national conversation**. Moreover, it got football connoisseurs across the world talking about India. I remember being in France and had people asking me about the ISL. There is definitely promise in the idea of the ISL, and I was amongst the first of the sceptics to voice my concerns. But, if the ISL can steer clear of corruption (a lot easier said than done in a country riddled by black markets), keep prices affordable to the masses, bring the beautiful game to forefront of the whole show and finally come good on its promises of grassroots involvement - then, it will silence its critics in the near future. It has already done a lot right up until now, like forcing clubs to improve their infrastructure, keeping ticket prices affordable and developing a fanbase for domestic football through professional broadcasting but needs to keep pushing in that direction. Perhaps the most important aspect will be the transition into a full-fledged league. The success of the 3-month edition is all good and well, but does that really mean anything?

## THE MERGER:

The existence of two separate leagues in Indian football cannot benefit anyone in truth. In December, the All India Football Federation general secretary, Kushal Das, announced plans of an ISL/I-League merger. There are a lot of problems that will come up in the merger but everyone linked to football in India knows that it is definitely a step in the right direction. Arunava Chaudhari, Mumbai FC's CEO, is convinced that this is progress. He believes that both the ISL and the I-League present strengths and weaknesses and a SWOT analysis of the each league needs to be done to define what the merger will entail. However, he is unsure whether this will happen. The reality is that the I-League has been around for quite a while now and hasn't really benefited Indian football much. The ISL only came into existence in 2014 and has really got people talking about Indian football. In its early stages the ISL was branded a "gimmick" and a "money making scheme", the footballing aspect of it was pushed to the back with the primary goal seemingly being profits. The merger is now the perfect opportunity for Indian football to kick on and combine a league that is an attractive financial proposition with something that will set the stage for Indian football to develop. The hope is that the merger will bring some clarity to Indian football as a whole with a defined calendar year so consumers can know what to expect. Undoubtedly, there will be tempers flaring between ISL and I-League clubs because legacy clubs that have been around for a while might have to suck it up and take a hit. Legacy clubs can be expected to take a back seat, and find themselves in the second tier of Indian football while ISL clubs come to fore. It will be hard to accept just because the I-League has been around for longer and is technically India's professional league but "this is something we have to do for the sake of Indian football" in the words of Kushal Das.

The cold hard truth is that the I-League has done little to improve the footballing landscape in India, while the ISL proved to be a hit from day one. The ISL accomplished a lot more in the 3 years it has been around than the I-League has done in just over 20 years. But, the ISL is a 3-month league. Convincing players to come spend 3-months in India at the swanky hotels of each of the country's biggest cities isn't too hard of a prospect. Getting them to commit to spending the entire year there and moving there permanently, though, is a whole other ball game. Most foreign ISL players wouldn't even bring their families with them the entire time. The transition is going to be important from a financial point of view too. The money players in the ISL were getting was unheard of in Indian football or any other league with comparable quality levels. Clubs could afford to pay the premium they had to in order to attract the talent to India because they only had to offer 3-month contracts. Once this needs to be extended to a minimum of 10-months, if monthly pay were to drop would the league be anywhere near as enticing to foreign talent?

There are a lot of questions that need to be answered and a lot of details that need to be looked at in the process of the merger. While announcing the merger is definitely a step in the right direction, the real work is yet to be done. The fine tuning of the plan may take a couple years to get right but it will all be worth it in the long term if things are done efficiently.

## THE NATIONAL TEAM:

While there are clearly positive signs in Indian football, the state of the national team is usually a very good way to judge the global state of football in a country. As of today, India sit 135th in the FIFA rankings sandwiched between Vietnam and Sudan. Unfortunately, any progression that has been made in Indian football has yet to be reflected on its national team which lost 7 of its 8 qualification matches for the World Cup in 2020. Clubs that come into the Indian market looking to develop their brand name and help develop the sport in India today, aren't doing so with the immediate intention of scouting talent. Right now, their goal is to develop a following for their club and to bring football to the country as a whole. It is not a talent identification exercise because the game isn't as widely developed as it needs to be (yet) in the entire country. Clubs that come into the Indian market are there for the long term, it is not just a week or two stay - it has got to be a long term initiative to develop the game at the grassroots level. India cannot expect to qualify for a World Cup until it has qualified for an Under 17 World Cup, an Under 19 World Cup and an Under 21 World Cup. Each of these are necessary steps. The same way a business can't shoot for a million dollars in revenue without first achieving a thousand, then ten thousand and so on. But, the people involved in, and at the head of, Indian football today, aren't necessarily too keen on the long game. And this is where the main problem with Indian football is currently - there are too many different actors involved that are looking for short term profits rather than looking to a long term development strategy. The people with the skin in the game are hesitant to put down any money without any instant profits, and this is understandable. But, the first and most important thing that needs to happen is that there needs to be a single, unified vision to develop football in India. Once this is in place the benefits will begin to show in the coming years.

It's definitely not all negative though. India is hosting the 2017 Under 17 World Cup, therefore awarding the Indian U17 side automatic qualification to the tournament - a great opportunity for India both from a footballing side and the organisational side. Firstly, it will give Indian kids the opportunity to impress. From the outside, there will be next to no expectations from the Indian outfit at the tournament, and the kids playing have nothing to lose. If they can go and put on a decent show who knows which clubs might look to sign a couple of them. It will also give the AIFF a chance to see just how far behind other countries India is at the developmental stage. From an organisational perspective, hosting a FIFA tournament is huge. It will force India to further develop its infrastructure, maintain it and give the country some experience in hosting such an event. FIFA laws stipulate that a country must have hosted a worldwide event before it can host a FIFA World Cup. Hosting this tournament now makes India eligible to host a proper World Cup, a prospect that will surely have millions of Indians licking their lips.

### TAKEAWAY:

- Currently, there is no definition to Indian football - it is a complete an utter mess.
- The ISL has brought fresh hope to Indian football and this is the perfect opportunity to kickstart things.
- The initial success of the ISL hasn't been reproduced in the third season but the picture isn't that clear cut, and it is not all negative.
- The announced merger will be key in defining the next few years of football in India and is a massive step in the right direction. There needs to be a movement a way from the "gimmicky" aspect of the ISL and more towards a traditional league.
- Along with the merger, the creation of youth leagues are the two things that need to be on the top of the AIFF's list of priorities.

# CHAPTER 4

# TAILORING TO FIT

———

*"We see resistance in many parts of the world, but there are a lot of places in the world which are a lot harder to do business than in India,"*

TRAVIS KALANICK, UBER CEO

Tony Pulis is no short of a cult figure in English football. Today, he is the manager of West Bromwich Albion as they enjoy one of their most successful Premier League seasons to date. Pulis is known for his unblemished record in the Premier League having never been relegated as well as his simplistic view on football. During Pulis' time at Stoke City, he took what was a very average team and made them one of the most feared teams in the league amongst giants like Manchester United, Chelsea, Arsenal and Liverpool. Given their financial constraints and the quality of their squad, Stoke was a team that was expected to find themselves in a relegation scrap every season. In the Welshman's seven year stint at the club, not once did his team find themselves outside of the top division. What he did was he turned the Britannia Stadium, Stoke's home venue, into a fortress.

*The instant when Rory Delap's long throw was nodded home by Mama Sidibe for a 94th-minute winner at the end of the Britannia's very first Premier League fixture in August 2008...*

If there is one single moment to define Stoke's fortress it would be that one. The sloped pitch, and rainy/cold conditions at Stoke were often unbearable. You could look at that as a negative but Pulis used it to his team's advantage. He knew that he would play 19 home games (at the Brittania) a season while their opponents would each only play once at the venue. Stoke used the blustery, freezing conditions to their advantage with their long-ball, tough-tackling and old-fashioned approach to the game. That is what made the Britannia Stadium one of the hardest places to go to in the Premier League. What Pulis did was he adapted the game to everything he had at his disposal and made the best of it; he turned his weaknesses into his strengths. The phrase, "but could you do it on a cold, rainy Tuesday night away at Stoke?" (meaning could you do it in the toughest conditions possible) was used by just about every fan in English football at one point.

India needs to do something similar. Football is one thing that most countries in this world have in common yet, football means something different in each one of these countries. India needs to adapt the game to their culture and turn their weaknesses into strengths. The ISL is the perfect example of adapting something for it to work in India. Even though, the critics aren't too happy about the ISL being a "tamasha", that is just the way that things have to be - at least at the start - for the sport to start gaining traction and making space for itself. Football is not the same in any two countries. The game is adapted to fit in with the culture, the mentality of the people comes across in the way the game is played. Football in Brazil, is like a dance - you hear about the "joga bonito" which translates to beautiful game - football is all about style, rhythm and showboating in Brazil. If you watch world superstar Neymar in his early days, he would be dancing around with the ball in the classic all-white Santos kit. If he tried the same thing in England, he would not last a second. A big stocky defender would fly in with a two-footed tackle leaving him for dead. English football is all about tenacity and winning, it doesn't matter how you do it but you've got to win. In fact, the dirtier and the more aggressive the better. In Spain, it's all about the passing and the intricate details. Even if teams are set up to play against the likes of Barcelona and Real Madrid they will never look to play defensive football and grind out a draw. They will set up the same way, never letting the opponent affect their philosophy of play...

Each population adapts the game to their strengths and uses everything they have in their arsenal to become better. India is one of the most unique countries in the world and needs to start playing the beautiful game to the tune of it's culture - as it is doing in other industries like the taxi one...

## UBER:

Football isn't the only thing that has to adapt to succeed in India. Some of the biggest and most successful brands realised that their approach to India as a market was going to have to be adapted to its unique qualities. While their new and original business plans might have fit and had unparalleled success elsewhere but, India posed a very different problem to the market. Take the example of Uber, arguably one of the biggest and best start ups in the last 10 years. Uber came into the Indian market a few years ago and realised that what they had been selling themselves on in the US - a cash-free payment method for transportation - was never going to work in one of the most cash-friendly economies in the world. In America, Uber rides became synonymous with never having to pull out your wallet again but this was a strategy that could never work in India. In a country where credit card penetration is in the low single digit percentages, Travis Kalanick (Uber's CEO) realised that offering cash as a payment method was a necessity. "You have to be empathetic to reality. You can bend reality but you cannot break it... We take cash in India.

We've always wanted to provide quality customer support and that's the only non-negotiable." Uber saw exponential growth in what is today their second largest market, outside of the US. They rose from a 13% market share in India, in terms of number of rides, in 2014 to a 30% market share by 2016. Uber recognised that this growth was only the first step towards success in India and by no means guaranteed profits. In fact, the San Francisco based company is still running at a loss in India because they are being forced to spend big in order to acquire customers. The taxi market in India is expected to stand at $36 billion by 2020 and despite all the positives, Uber still plays second fiddle to local player Ola, which has a near 50% market share. The executives know that the need to localise, without diluting their brand, is crucial and this has led to the launch of UberMOTO in India. Rapid urbanisation, a growing young population and limited public transportation options all add up to create a huge yet unmet demand. Uber saw just how essential tailoring itself to fit India is in their attempt to taste success in the world's fastest growing economy. Amazon, too, was faced with a number of competitors in the Indian market and was also forced to adapt its uniqueness. Amazon offers cash on delivery, something that was thought to be way too risky in delivery yet turned out to be a non-negotiable in India. Today, Amazon enjoys great success in India and is continuing to grow.

## ISL:

The ISL is a step in the right direction because it really brings out the essence of India with the big bash mentality. It followed in the steps of India's premier domestic cricket league, the Indian Premier League (IPL). The IPL is the possibly the greatest success story in domestic Indian sports. The IPL took the "gentlemen's game" and put a Bollywood twist on it. The organisers took cricket, and tailored it to their consumers tastes. They brought in the perfect amount of stardust. Paired it with the right investors and the ideal format to make the most successful cricket league that has ever existed. The game just became a lot more exciting where each game was an entire event on its own; with cheerleaders and music. The IPL made cricket the most glamorous and luxurious prospect it could possibly be. The tournament attracts the best players from all over the world and has completely changed the whole landscape of cricket in the world. The IPL is now the most elite competition of the cricket calendar year... Nowadays, players even turn down opportunities to play for their countries so that they can participate in the Indian tournament. While the IPL is known to be a great business prospect, with everyone involved raking in the profits, it has also benefited Indian cricket greatly. Indian cricket now dominate the world... The Board of Control for Cricket in India (BCCI) is bigger than the International Cricket Council (ICC). There are even rumours that the ICC "tampered with" the draw for the World Cup to favour India because, in terms of viewership, India represents 70% of the ICC's revenue. Not only did the league really become a success in terms or number of followers and profits, it also helped improve the standards of cricket in India. The IPL required that teams play young and exciting new Indian talents. They limited the number of foreigners that each team was allowed to field and this led to a much larger talent pool for the national team selectors to pick from.

Of course, this success story can only take place because cricket is so widely developed across India. Nevertheless it is proof that India is suited to great sport leagues if the fine-tuning is done right.

Indian football as a whole needs to embrace a certain footballing culture that bodes well with other cultural aspects of the country. Coaches and players will come and go but there needs to be a certain sense of continuity that this culture will establish. There needs to be a long-term cohesive goal that is both realistic and tailored to India. There are currently, a lot of different projects going on in India to promote and develop football. The problem isn't necessarily that they are going in the wrong direction, it is that they aren't going in the same direction. They need to be playing to their strengths rather than their weaknesses. The Indian cricket team has realised and accepted that they aren't going to be the biggest and strongest athletes out there, but this doesn't mean that they just throw in the towel and accept defeat. No. They take it on the chin and make sure they overcompensate for the weakness by being the smartest, most technical and hardest working players. Just like Uber was "empathetic to reality" and has managed to localise themselves to India "without diluting their brand". This points to another necessity for Indian clubs. While they might have to focus on bringing foreigners into India to improve the level of the league, they can't treat them differently to the Indians. At the end of the day, the Indians are the ones in their own country and while they should learn from the experiences of the foreign players - things should be tailored to India. The best clubs in the world recruit players from all over the world, but once they arrive in a new country they are forced to learn the language and to adapt to the new culture. There is no reason why Indian clubs shouldn't expect the same from the foreigners in their squads. Learning Hindi and understanding the Indian culture can only help because the more comfortable everyone feels, the easier it will be for them to perform on the pitch. And in the long run Indian football needs to maintain its "Indian-ness".

*One step back, and two steps forward.*

Going back to the Uber example. Before Uber came into the Indian taxi market they couldn't have the same impact they had in other countries because they had a direct competitor other than just local government sanctioned taxis. Ola was, and remains, the biggest player in the taxi space in India. Just like any other business, Uber's primary goal is always going to be to maximise profits - that is the definition of capitalism and it's not going to change anytime soon. But, Uber realised that to set themselves up for the long term, they had to take a loss and forego profits in the near future. They realised that they had to establish their brand name and establish themselves as big players in the market. Their initial goal was to eat up the market and gain a considerable share in the shortest time period possible by undercutting prices massively. Sure enough, they executed their plan and after steady price hikes - all whilst maintaining constant growth in market share - Uber are close to being front runners in the market. The step back for Uber was the initial losses they faced in the first few months. Once they established themselves in the market though, they took their two steps forward. Now, Uber is very well set up in India and can expect to rake in the profits for the foreseeable future.

The ISL needs to serve as the sort of short term fix for Indian football. While it is an attractive proposition and has developed a following for domestic football in India, the structure of it is not going to help the development of the sport in the long term. The same way Uber had to cut prices and accept losses in their early stages to gain market share, we have to accept that a league like the ISL where football may not be at the centre of things is a necessary evil to build the fanbase for the sport. Only once there is a large base of consumers can the sport develop - because there has to be a demand for it to develop. Take cricket as an example, if the Indian cricket board screws up something no one is going to stand for it because of the importance of the game in India. There has to be a consumer movement to demand a change in the current situation of football. But, there has to be a clear set of goals in place for a number of viewers to hit and a number of professional players to hit, for example. The ISL cannot be the finished product. It is definitely a great start to an adaptation of a football league in India as well as one that has already began to attract attention throughout the world. Yet, there are tons of modifications that still need to be made for it to aid the true development of the sport rather than just the size of the fanbase. Once numbers are hit there has to be a transition to a league that will benefit football in the long term, just like the way Uber raised prices steadily to maintain the growth in market share. There needs to be a movement towards a set up that will benefit Indian talent and India as a whole rather than a "gimmicky" league. Not to take anything away from the ISL, because it is definitely helping Indian football in more ways than one! At the same time though, for football to kick on after this first phase, a lot has to be done in the background to set things up. This goes back to the **two pillars** of developing any sport any where: **grassroots** and **infrastructure**. And this needs to happen now. Because, these are the two key areas that need to be the focus. During the interviews I held, each and every person stated that these are the two areas that need to be emphasised on in order to develop the sport in India.

## CHINA:

India's next-door-neighbours are the perfect example of developing a sport on the two pillars (grassroots and infrastructure) with a single unified vision. China is similar to India in the fact that it is one of the fastest growing economies in the world, and that it has a mammoth-sized population. 10 years ago, Chinese football wasn't all that developed either. But, what put the east Asian country lightyears ahead of India today?

Initially, China's strategy was to handpick 200-300 young players a year and send them abroad to clubs in Europe. The thought behind this was that they develop faster if they were learning from the best. The program was set up in a way so that the players would be put in some of the best academies in the world, understand the game better than they would have ever done in their own country and return home full of knowledge and talent. The problem was that the players would come back and not do all that well for a variety of different reasons. In the case of Dong Fangzhou - the first and only Chinese footballer to have played for Manchester United till date - he came back to China after things didn't quite work out in Europe for him. He came back with the thought that he had been playing in China would be a walk in the park given that he had spent his last few years playing with the some of the world's best. Sadly, things went from bad to worse for him and he saw himself not making the first team squad on most occasions and getting out of shape. He had gone from being the man who could have been a trailblazer in Chinese football - the sports equivalent to Yao Ming - to a **no one**. Things went as far as Fangzhou becoming a mockery on Chinese reality shows.

This is just one story, but globally over ten years there were no big success stories coming out of this model. Players would come back to China and just couldn't perform for different reasons.

Then, a couple of years ago, they decided to change their model. In 2013, President Xi Jinping rose to power and demanded that China become a world footballing power. He set out a mandate to completely rebuild the sport from the grassroots level through to hosting and, even winning, the World Cup. His obsession with the game and the Chinese political system coupled to attract millions of dollars to the game. All those who wanted and needed to be in the good books of the government (so literally everyone) began to invest in the game. The new, and current, strategy was two-fold:

1.   Establish a proper grassroots system in the country to churn out world class talent for the years to come.
2.   Develop the domestic league in hopes of making it one of best in the world.

Until this strategy was put in place. Chinese football wasn't exactly the best in the world. Firstly, the grassroots programs in China were fairly lacklustre. The strategy of sending players abroad was a program that would help only the top few players rather than raising the level of the entire country. But, once the people in power came to the realisation that the current system didn't seem to be working too well they knew they had to shake things up. So, the Chinese put a plan in place with lots of different moving parts but the most important part was the starting point. In Malcolm Gladwell's book, Outliers, he speaks of the relative age effect. The relative age effect is a phenomenon that suggests that there is a bias (present in most youth sports) in favour of athletes born in the first three months of the year. Players are compared to others of the same age - so everyone born in the same year will compete for a set number of spots. The problem with this is that at the ripe young age of 5 or 6, a few months of maturity (both mental and physical but predominantly the latter) are that much more obvious and valuable. Therefore, such a minuscule will influence decisions on picking the best players. A study conducted amongst the elite youth teams of Spain, looking for such trends in the birth months of players, found that 48% of the players were born in the first quarter of the year while only 9% were born in the last quarter. January was the most popular birth month with 18% of players while December was the least popular with a mere 0.2%. Given that child births are fairly evenly distributed across the year with spikes in July through September and lows in January, February and April

- it is clear that there is a bias towards players born earlier in the year because they have had a little more time to develop. These players are shown favouritism from a young age and the snowball effect of the advantages only accentuates this phenomenon. So, the youth players that the Chinese federation were sponsoring to go abroad might not have even been the best players in the country for their age.

So China, knew that they needed to do something different to succeed; so they looked to their strengths. With the biggest population in the world, China used their strength in numbers to their advantage. Rather than selecting the best few players and specifically training them to become better, they are working on making the worst players better. While this might sound counter productive and just plain stupid if you take a second to think about it, it makes a lot more sense. Instead of just making a handful of players better they are making the entire football-playing Chinese population better. By improving the level of the worst player you are inadvertently making the best players better because you are increasing the level of competition. If the worst players are becoming better, this will force the average players to become better too because there is more competition. If they don't then they, now, become the worst players. This trend continues upwards and the best players now have to push themselves to be better or risk not being amongst the best anymore. It's like pushing up the whole block rather than pushing apart pieces of the block to increase the differences. Not only does this method improve the overall level of the sport in the country, it also grows the talent pool that selectors can choose from. This is the way the federation had to work to bring the game to the stage it is at today. Understandably, they are still going to have to select the best players from age groups to really buckle down on and expend time and money on to make them the country's best players. But the "making the worst better" strategy improved the overall level of the game, which helped in making up the difference in development between China and their European or South American counterparts in football.

The second part of the plan, is one that has really come into the limelight ever since the 2016 summer transfer window (and even more so in the 2017 January window). Developing the domestic league is key in developing domestic talent, and this is what China have begun to do in recent years. Today, managers as high-profile as Arsene Wenger (manager of Arsenal) and Rafa Benitez (manager of Newcastle United) are saying that the Chinese Super League is beginning to become a threat to European football. The highest paid players in world football no longer play for Real Madrid or Manchester United, now they play for Shanghai SIPG, Guangzhou Evergrande and Shanghai Shenhua. China as a whole has thrown money the way of players and attracted them to their domestic league. The goal in bringing some of the biggest names in world football to China is to entice the kids to play football and start a generational movement towards developing the sport in China. And the Chinese can do this because everyone involved in the sport is on the same page (also having billions of dollars to throw around doesn't hurt their case). The money the Chinese clubs are offering is quite simply stupendous. 6 players have moved to the Chinese Super League for fees of $50 million or more, and 5 of the 8 highest paid players in world football now play in the Chinese Super League. The league has managed to attract some of the top players in world football purely because of the money. Axel Witsel, a former Zenit St. Petersburg player, had the option to move to China or to one of the biggest and most historic clubs in the sport, Juventus.

Guess which one he chose.

China, because "it was an offer I just could not turn down" (as a quick side-note, I respect his honesty because other players who claim it has always been their dream to play in China - that is complete bullshit). Real Madrid were reportedly offered just over $300 million for the services of Cristiano Ronaldo but the player refused the transfer. This move would have made Ronaldo the highest earning player in the game but for now Carlos Tevez occupies that position earning over $40 million a year.

Recent events have led to Chelsea manager, Antonio Conte, expressing his fear of the "danger" of the Chinese buying power and the effect it will have on the competitive spirit of the game. In fact, the Chinese league has got so much publicity that the so-called broadcasting 'home of sport' in England, Sky Sports, will be showing the Chinese league.

Money is no more than an object right now in Chinese football and developing their league will surely benefit the national team in the near future. It is important to note though, that China has put in some measures to keep an emphasis on developing domestic talent. While the foreigners and big names of the game might be at center stage, there has to be a constant emphasis on Chinese talent. A rule allowing each team to field only 4 foreign players as well as the fact that foreign goalkeepers are banned from the league continues to help develop Chinese talent. In fact, the government have even stepped in to enforce laws reducing spending on players in the Chinese league.

The second stage of development has really put China in the spotlight but all this is only possible because of the framework that the first stage put in place. Initially, all the money was going into grassroots and infrastructure - this is what set the stage for the federation to really push on and develop the sport at the top level.

China tailored the development of the game to their country. They took advantage of its mammoth-sized population by raising the overall level of the game with the "making the worst better" strategy from the previous chapter. The way drills were being run at academies and schools throughout the country was so innovative and original. You would never dream of seeing stuff like that in Europe. 300 kids would be on a single football pitch running drills, the precision of timing and attention to detail was comparable to the navy seals. Football training was military-like in China because it could be. It matched the Chinese traits of obedience and discipline.

**India needs to learn.** Indian football has got to create an identity for itself that fits with its rich history and culture.

### NATIONAL TEAM:

The Indian national team needs to adapt to its own culture and conditions. The national team has never reached the heights you would expect the second most populous country in the world to attain. There isn't any real style to the play and no recognisable tactics generally speaking. Tough conditions have been an excuse that a lot of people have turned to in order to explain the lack of success India has had in football. In truth though, the tough conditions should be used to India's advantage.

In 2007 FIFA banned international matches from being played at more than 2,500 metres above sea level. They claimed "the decision was made due to concerns over players' health and possible distortion of competition". The ban was met with fury in Latin America, notably from Bolivia who play their home matches in La Paz at an altitude of 3,600m above sea level. Evo Morales, Bolivia's president, vowed to lead a campaign against the ruling and said that the ban was a clear example of discrimination. Many claim that the ban came on the back of constant pressure from Brazil and Argentina, South America's two major football powers, given that they had both struggled to get results in these conditions. Fast forward to May 2008 to when the ban was lifted after a letter of protest from the governing body of South American football (CONMEBOL). Bolivia, along with Peru and Ecuador, were allowed to return to their previous home grounds for international matches. To this day, some of the best players in the world struggle to cope with conditions in the Bolivian capital of La Paz. Bolivia don't boast of one of the stronger sides in Latin American football but, when games in La Paz are tight, more often than not things swing in the favour of the home side. There are famous scenes of footballing god Leo Messi vomiting on the pitch because he just can't handle the thin air. Ecuador are an even better example. They too play their games in high altitude and today find themselves third in the qualifying group for the 2018 World Cup, ahead of the likes of Chile, Argentina and Colombia.

India needs to take a page out of Bolivia or Ecuador's books and take advantage of the fact that they **can** acclimatise themselves to tough conditions like the burning heat, the torrentuous downpours or the high-altitude whilst others just **cannot**. The same way Stoke City knew the way the wind, rain and slope would affect play India needs to master their conditions. This way they can gain a massive advantage on home ground and give themselves chances of beating teams that might be better than them.

**TAKEAWAY:**

- India needs to make football Indian - adapt football to fit India and play the game in a way unique to its own culture.
- For this to happen there needs to be a defined identity for the sport in India as well as a unified goal for all parties involved in the game.

# PART 3

# CREATING A PLATFORM FOR FOOTBALL IN INDIA

In Million Dollar Arm, the scouting process included hiring a judge of talent and setting up pitching nets in various parts of the country. It was fairly easy because it included just one motion and this dumbed down the process quite a bit. In football, however, the process could never be that easy because so many different aspects come into play when judging a player's potential. This is why finding the talent in India is one of the hardest steps in the process of developing the sport. But, the same way there is a whole infrastructure for talent spotting in football in Europe, talented cricket players in India have the scope to be found. You can be in the most remote village in the country, but if you are talented one way or another the word will get out. You will then proceed to representing your school in tournaments, before representing your state in nationwide tournaments and finally you will don the country's colours at international events. There needs to be a platform put in place for talented players to be able to have somewhere to demonstrate their talent and know this will take them somewhere. An integral part in setting up this platform, is changing the approach to football in India. Football needs to be a sport that can appeal to the whole country, to the masses. Football isn't perceived as a career in India and this is because of the role that the sport plays. In a few parts of the country, football is a real part of the culture. But, it really isn't the dominant sport for the country as a whole and it is not what most kids dream of from a young age. Until there are a couple success stories, this perception wont change because it isn't a path that has been walked before. In Africa, Europe and, Latin America, kids that come from poverty know that football can be a route out of their situations because some of their heroes were trailblazers and set the example.

# CHAPTER 5

# CHANGING THE APPROACH

———

*"Here it is cricket, cricket and cricket; and second is football. Cricket is a religion here but football is a way of life. The passion for football, especially in Kolkata and West Bengal, in Goa and Mumbai and in the north-east, is beyond imagination. It's a morning ritual – at the breakfast table there is a discussion about football,"*

UTSAV PAREKH IN SAPTARSHI RAY'S
ARTICLE, THE GUARDIAN

Cristiano Ronaldo and Lionel Messi are without a doubt the two best footballers today. Many believe that they are the two best football players of all time. But, the path to success wasn't simple for either of the two.

**Cristiano Ronaldo:** Cristiano Ronaldo is the poster boy of football. He is the reason a lot people love football - the reason that girls love, or rather don't mind, watching football and the reason boys change their haircuts. Most of all though, Cristiano Ronaldo is the best rags-to-riches story sports has seen. Born on the 5th of February, 1985 in Madeira, Cristiano was the youngest of four children. His parents planned to get an abortion because they were struggling to support a family for five and the prospect of having a sixth mouth to feed and a sixth set of bills to pay weren't an option that Cristiano's parents could entertain. Fortunately, they never followed through with these plans. Life wasn't easy for Cristiano though. The son of a cook and a gardener was never expected to lead a luxurious; stardom was nothing but a distant dream. Football was more than a passion, though, for the Portuguese captain. It was a path out of poverty and something that he had to be the best at. Ever since a young age, Cristiano was, and still is, known to be the hardest working player. First in and last out at training on a daily basis. The epitome of a perfectionist. After proving himself and putting a number of Portuguese clubs to shame during spells at Andorinha and CD Nacional, Sporting Lisbon offered Ronaldo a contract. At this time, little did he know that this was only the platform that would lead to bigger and better things. In just one season Ronaldo moved up through the ranks through the Under 17s, Under 18s, and the Reserves into the First Team. The moment of magic that led to everything that was to come, was during a friendly against the mighty Manchester United.

"It was in the first half when he made the run, inside John O'Shea. And I thought 'bloody hell'. When you're watching a player who you would usually play against, you look much more closely and it's very rare to see that level of movement and speed. Only a few people are capable of timing a run like that, inside the full-back and centre back - and the speed of it."

These are the words of Gary Neville, Manchester United's right-back at the time. Cristiano Ronaldo had absolutely terrorised one of Europe's best defences and left them with nightmares. Many claim that the United players urged Sir Alex Ferguson to sign him at half-time. While a manager of Sir Alex's calibre probably wouldn't have just signed a player based on 45-minutes of football, Ronaldo made his Manchester United debut in front of 67,000 people against Bolton Wanderers just a few months later.

Today, Cristiano Ronaldo is considered by many to be the world's best player and is also the all-time top goalscorer for both club and country.

**Lionel Messi:** 1983 marked the end of the "Dirty War" and the return to democracy in Argentina. In 1987, Argentina were the reigning world champions and the home to the best footballer at the time, a certain Diego Maradona. But, 1987 was marked by the birth of a footballing genius - Lionel Messi. As the son of a steel worker and a cleaner in a poor part of Rosario, Lionel Messi lead a very simple life. He inherited his father's love and passion for the beautiful game and was an absolute addict.

"When his mother sent him off to run errands, Leo always took his football with him. And if he didn't have one, he would make one out of plastic bags or socks."

The struggle furthered however, when, at the ripe age of 11, Leo and his parents found out that he was suffering from a growth hormone deficiency and without treatment, his dreams of becoming a professional footballer would be out of reach. His parents were barely surviving on the money they were making and struggled to make ends meet. His father believed his son's footballing talent could lead to financial help. After discussions with River Plate and Newell's Old Boys, two of Argentina's most historic clubs, didn't lead to anything concrete the situation didn't look like it was going to get any better. The reception of an impressive video of Leo Messi juggling an orange (113 times in a row) and a tennis ball (120 times in a row) at FC Barcelona led to him being invited for a trial with the Spanish giants. Eventually, Leo Messi became an official FC Barcelona player as they agreed to pay for his treatment as well as offering him a contract with a salary capable of supporting his entire family.

A decade later, Leo Messi is a five-time Ballon d'Or winner (the Best Footballer of the Year award), and also the all-time top goalscorer for both club and country.

Messi and Ronaldo provided sports with two of the most inspiring storylines it has ever known. Two young boys, from families who were struggling to put food on the table at the end of each day became the two most decorated individual footballers of all time. But, this only happened because of the role and the approach to the beautiful game in their respective countries. The two players depended on football to earn a living and were even supporting their entire families before their teenage years. Football wasn't just a sport, a hobby or even a passion for both Leo Messi and Cristiano Ronaldo, it was a necessity. Football represented a path out of poverty and the start to a new life. Talent definitely played a big part in the successes of both men, but their unquestionable and relentless dedication to the sport is what brought them to the points they find themselves at today; the top.

The role of football, or the approach towards football in India is just not the same. Even though there is a strong, and developing, following of the game the same importance isn't given to the sport. Indian football doesn't have the same glitz and glamour as it does in the rest of the world, cricket occupies that spot! Yes, football isn't the number one sport in India but in a country with a population of over a billion there is potential for more than one sport to be developed. For India to progress and be able to compete on the world stage of football, the country's attitude towards football needs to change. It cannot be a mere "sofa-sport" in the majority of the country, football needs to become more than a hobby in India.

## DEMOGRAPHIC:

The first thing that needs to change in regards of the approach to the sport of football in India has to be the demographic of its fans. Football in India, is currently an urban sport that appeals mostly to the well-to-do families and more specifically to men between the ages of 16 and 25. While this has begun to change, the sport continues to draw the vast majority of its fans from big cities. This is why Mumbai, New Delhi, and Bangalore have become hotbeds for football. But, this isn't completely true and in speaking to Saptarshi Ray, a journalist for the Guardian, he took issue with this overview. "It really depends where you go in India, in parts of India like Kolkata, or places in the northeast like Assam and Sikkim football really is a way of life." He recalled visiting India as a child and the first thing his cousins in his hometown of Kolkata always wanted to do was play football. He argued that the "small" pockets in which football really is a part of the culture really aren't that small at all. "You've got enough people in these parts to stock your national team 50 times over!"

The biggest difference between the popularity of football in the big metropolitan cities of India and the so called "pockets of promise" is the role of the game. In the bigger cities, football has a fairly strong following. Every Saturday and Sunday, there will be people who plan their schedules around Premier League and La Liga kick off times and you'll spot the occasional kick about on the weekend. Football is more a spectator sport than a sport that people will actively play. In West Bengal, Goa and the northeast as a whole, though, football is just what you would picture it being like in Brazil. You can walk into any part and you will see kids barefoot in sandy fields kicking a ball about. It is a sport that captivates everyone, of all shapes and sizes.

Admittedly, the locals in these areas are nowhere near as talented as some of the masters you can find in the favelas in Sao Paulo or along Ipanema beach in Rio - but the culture is very similar. People fail to believe that there is a support culture for football. Yes, cricket is undoubtedly the top dog in India and nothing can rival it (for now at least). But, that is what football needs to understand. We're not, and we cannot, be trying to take on cricket. It would take a real idiot to try and take on cricket in India right now. What we need to be doing though is tapping into the underlying culture of football and this has to start in the parts of the country where the love for football is already established. These are densely populated parts of the country and the head start of football being engrained into the culture will lead to a shorter path to success. The best players in the world don't usually come from the big cities, but in their countries there is a way of being scouted even if you're in the most remote of places - just like with cricket in India.

In terms of changing the demographic of the game, India needs to concentrate its resources on the "pockets of promise" because these regions have a head start in the game. But, it is important to make football a sport that will appeal to the masses. That is what the game has defined itself on, and what it is all about across the entire world. Rags-to-riches story are the bread and butter of football. You look at all the top players in the world and the majority come from very modest beginnings. Football is a bigger part of their lives, in the extreme cases it is their route out of poverty but in less extreme cases sports are the only form of entertainment they can afford. This gives football such a big fanbase and such a big importance in countries like Germany and England - where football really is a lot, lot more than just a game.

**"I'm Palace till I die. I'm Palace till I die. I know I am, I'm sure I am; I'm Palace till I die."**

These were the words that rang around Selhurst Park in Croydon, a Southeastern suburb of London, on the 1st of June in 2010. Throngs of blue and red gathered around the stadium.

Men, women and children chanted outside the stadium in what resembled the holy pilgrimage to Mecca. Crystal Palace had been placed in administration and had until 3pm to find an investor or face liquidation. Crowds were chanting and praying for help to save their team - something that had come to resemble a family more than a sports team. Fans were desperate for help, they couldn't bare to see their beloved Crystal Palace disappear. Nothing else mattered to them at that point, just their team and the hope of a saving grace rescuing them from the point of no return. Mistakes from the club's moneymen had put them in a situation where they needed an investor to come in and pick up the pieces or risk losing everything they had ever known. Locals knew what a big role the club played in the area. Whether you like football or not, it is what defines the mood in Croydon. An area that is known for its danger, where all the doom and gloom just seemed to disappear for a few short hours on the weekend when Palace were in action. A win would lengthen the stay of happiness, but even with a loss it wasn't all gone. The area really just thrived on the success of the club, and losing it would have meant a whole lot more than one could imagine.

The point of all this, is that the role of football in England, as well as lots and lots of other countries, is monumental and purely indescribable. And while one might not associate that with India, the truth is that in the small pockets where the sport is really king it is quite similar. Kolkata derbies used to be the biggest days in Indian football. A match between the two powerhouses of the country, the two most historic teams in India - East Bengal and Mohun Bagan. Tempers would flare and the stadium (with a capacity of 120,000) would be packed to the rafters. So, the obsession for football is present in parts of India - it is about tapping into this and spreading it.

## RISE OF CRICKET:

Based on the current state of affairs in India today, it may be hard for some to believe that cricket hasn't always sat at the top of the food chain of Indian sports. In fact, until the 1980's cricket was barely even on the radar. Hockey is supposed to be India's national sport, but you'd be hard pushed to find a single Indian that knows this fact and would agree with it. However, India used to be a powerhouse in hockey. With 8 golds, 1 silver and 2 bronzes in the sport, India is, to this day, the most successful Olympic team in the sport! India basically monopolised the hockey gold medal at the Olympic games winning it 6 times in a row between 1928 and 1956. The national team maintained high-standards with podium finishes all the way through to 1972 and won their last gold medal in hockey at the 1980 Olympics. Since then though, it all went downhill for Indian hockey. The game had evolved and India got left behind. New methods were introduced to the game but the Indians were purists and weren't prepared to give up their traditional methods for success. This opened up the door to cricket.

Up until this point, cricket hadn't really enjoyed much success in India. The first ever test match was played in 1932 in which India lost to the almighty Australians. It wasn't till 20 years later that India finally won their first ever game of cricket. Fast forward to 1983, when India won the Cricket World Cup and this really started the boom. Obviously, things were on the right track before the tournament or they never would have won it. But, things just kept getting better after that. India had a strangle-hold on the world cricket scene with the likes of Sunil Gavaskar, and Kapil Dev initially guiding the country to the top. The torch was passed on to the god-like figure of Sachin Tendulkar, the ever-dependable Rahul Dravid and others. India had found a new form of entertainment (in cricket) to replace the sport that had lost its way. One of the most crucial aspects of crickets uprising was the introduction of television. What cricket had that hockey didn't was television coverage. It allowed everyone in India to follow the country's supremacy while hockey didn't. The truth is that India is still very much at the top of world cricket, but the game is definitely changing. There has been a big shift to a more physical game - with players more visibly fit across the game, something that not all Indian players seem to have kept up with. The legends of the game have retired, and there just aren't any real god-like figures in the Indian national team.

Are the wheels set in motion for new sports to come and challenge for the title of king sport in India? Well, as much as I'd love to say yes - the answer isn't that clear cut. As I have said taking on cricket in India would be crazy right now, but developing other sports and getting them to a stage at which they can be ready to pounce on any failures of cricket is definitely a good plan. It is hard to say cricket is on the down because financially speaking, the sport is almost nothing without India. But, it is clear to see that the game is changing and the cricket we see today is going further and further from the pure form of the sport. And, with some of the biggest clubs in world football opening up academies or starting other projects in India, football in India is definitely on the up. The ISL has begun a movement, there are more and more followers of football in the country and FIFA is looking to develop the sport in India! India is all set to host the 2017 Under 17 Football World Cup and this could be the start of something bigger.

**RISE OF NEW SPORTS:**

With the stage all set for a new sport to enter the market, it is essential that India changes its approach to sports other than cricket.

The approach to football needs to change for there to ever be a footballing revolution in India. The struggle to see football as a career by parents will continue until there are a few notable success stories in the sport. India is in the same position that countries like the US, Japan or Australia were 20-25 years ago, but today a World Cup without the likes of these countries is almost unthinkable. The trickle down effects of the development of the game are generational and won't come into play in the short run but that doesn't mean that they don't count.

This is why there needs to be a long-term vision and an integral part of it is the perception of the sport. Right now in India, sports are definitely a big part of the culture but the sporting culture in India is very different to that of the US or of England. In these countries, a career in sports is something that is fairly common and pretty viable. In India though, the only real sport that the country excels in right now is cricket. Education is so important to Indian parents and typically, sports just aren't a viable option to have a career in. This is because there is just no precedent of financial success in this field.

Given that a large part of the population lives in poverty, things only get harder. In the lower classes there are usually two different instances. There are the kids that are lucky enough to get an education, and they understand just how important it is for them to devote everything to this. They realise that this is a path that has been travelled before and one that can lead to them living a very different one to their parents'. And then, there are the children that aren't as lucky, and can't afford an education. They usually end up working from young ages. They either work to help their parents or work to earn money and help put food on the table at the end of the day. Sports, generally, are seen as a risk because of this. If you're spending time playing a sport that isn't guaranteed to lead to success then how can you substitute work or education for it? And this is why changing the approach to sports in India is going to be key to bring any sort of change to the footballing world. This isn't to say that kids from poor families or kids from the slums will never play football or cricket because they do. The difference is though, that they will play when they are growing up. But, once they "come of age" to start working or really need to start thinking about a career, well they just don't have the time for it anymore in their parents eyes because sports are just games. Kids that might have had the potential to be top athletes have to give up their dreams because it is too risky for them to give it a shot.

The positive is that this change is already in motion and the NBA is proof of this. You don't just see the NBA getting involved in anything and everything - the people that make the decisions there usually know what they are doing. The NBA has started to invest more and more in India, looking to unearth some Indian talent. They too realise the importance of changing the role of sports in India to bring a revolution to it. Eventually though, there is no better way to change the minds of people than by showing them proof. If India can create a big footballing star then surely there will be a long line of people to follow.

## STARTING FROM YOUNGER AGE:

Another integral part of sport in India is the age at which the kids who do have time for sports, begin to play properly. Tom Byer, a man widely known as the "Godfather of Japanese Football", was recently hired by the Chinese government to be the head of football development in the country. His vision of developing football is tried and tested, not only did it bring success to the men's national team in Japan but the women's team has reaped the benefits too. Tom's vision is that kids in Europe or South America develop an advantage from a very, very young age because football is a part of their culture and they are exposed to this before they can even walk. Between the ages of 2 and 6, children begin to develop their technical abilities. If a child makes a size 1 football their favourite toy and gets as many touches of the ball in as possible at a young age, by the time he gets on the pitch at age 6 they will already hold an advantage.

Coaching practices vary across the world, but it is not by chance that the countries with the most technically gifted players are the ones that focused on technique the most. In Holland, for example, kids in academies don't spend too much time running laps, doing sprints or even playing matches - most of their time is spent doing drills with the football. The goal behind this is for each individual child to get as many touches on the ball as possible. Building speed, stamina and tactical understanding for the game is important, no doubt, but this will come with time. Technique is what needs to be worked on the most. Rather than playing a match - where only one child will touch the ball at any given time - each player is given a ball and they are taught to run through drills with army-like precision. Series of passes and dribbles are combined. An integral part of Mr. Byer's philosophy is that football must have just as much, if not more, of an impact off the pitch as it does on and this requires the parents to get involved too. Given that Tom was looking to develop this method in Japan and China, two places where the mentality towards the game was different to what it is in India. This all needs to be adapted. First of all, in India it is not part of the culture for kids to spend time playing sports with their parents - you just won't see a son and his father throwing a baseball (or even a cricket ball) around in the backyard. Parents don't even usually help their own children with their homework. Typically kids get sent to tutors as early as at 10 years old. But, if there is a solution to this and Indian children to start to master manipulating a football by such a young age then surely we will have an Indian football revolution on our hands.

Starting to play the sport from a younger age and engraining it into the mind and culture of the children will benefit them in terms of technique, but not only. In the mid-2000's Darryl Duffy, a British striker, went from playing a bit-part role at League Two side Cheltenham to becoming the star-man at Salgaocar - one of India's top clubs. He had gone from warming the bench in the fourth division of English football to being one of the best players at the top level of Indian football (since then Indian football has definitely progressed but this gives you an idea of the way things used to be not too long ago). From the dirt roads, to the cows, to the stray dogs - everything seemed to shock the Brit in India.

On the football side though, he was surprised to see that there were lots of talented players. The biggest difference he saw between British and Indian players, though, was in the understanding of the game and the quickness of the minds. During my time at Metz, a handful of other Indians were brought to train with the French team for a couple of weeks. The plan was for each of the players to play with the corresponding Metz youth team of their age group during their stay. Once they arrived and got into the swing of things, they just couldn't cope. Physically it was too tough - but this was understandable, even some of the most talented players come to Europe and struggle physically in the beginning, Neymar is a great example. But, the speed of play and the speed of thinking was just a world apart. This is where my being brought up mostly in Europe helped me. When football is a part of your lifestyle and culture, and you start playing from a younger age things just come naturally. The current lack of qualified coaches and lack of youth leagues makes it hard for this to happen, but developing grassroots programs is promising. Creating leagues and academies needs to be high up on the list of priorities for things to do in order to really get football going in India.

## THE PROFESSIONAL GAME:

The overall lack of professionalism in football in India is astounding. Going into this summer working at Fateh Hyderabad, I wasn't expecting to glitz and glamour but nevertheless, I was just shocked. The bureaucracy, the lack of definition, the miscommunication, the infrastructure - everything was just shocking. Some say that the ISL has brought more professionalism into the sport and it does seem to be true, but there has only been a small change and there is a long way to go still. This brings me onto another problem though. The current set up of Indian football leagues doesn't help the situation too much either. Almost everyone I spoke to sees this as one of the biggest flaws in Indian football today - there needs to be a reference to a single competition and this is the real driver for any sport. No other country has various leagues that aren't affiliated in any way, and there is no reason that this should be the case in India. Plans to merge the two leagues (the I-League and the ISL) is definitely a step in the right direction and the way things pan out will depend on the new entity that is formed.

Another side is the professionalism in the day to day of clubs. Fitness is one area that footballers in India seem to lack.

Cricket might be able to bypass this because the sport isn't as physically demanding but, football just cannot. The average Indian diet is not as healthy as the average European diet and this difference is reproduced when it comes to sports. It was incredible because in conversations with some professional football players in India about hygiene and diet they just seemed completely clueless and unaware. It is hard to blame the players because they clearly haven't been educated on this. Some don't know any better because they hadn't been in the professional set up for long, but others had played for the national team and still didn't know that fried food is unhealthy. A Portuguese fitness trainer who has experience in the second division in Portugal was just appalled at the levels of fitness and knowledge Indian players seemed to have. While this was just a first impression based on a group of 25 trialists, some of the players in the group had played for I-League teams and others had been at some of the best academies in the country. The players aren't to blame for this because they just weren't taught any better and this needs to change. There needs to be a better understanding from a younger age as well.

## TAKEAWAY:

- Demographic of football fans in India as a whole needs to change from just the urban middle class to the masses as well.
- There is an underlying culture of football in India, specifically in the "pockets of promise"

- There are parts of India (Goa, Kolkata, North East) where football is king and these are the parts where resources should be focused initially
- Starting to play the sport from a younger age is essential in developing a better understanding of the game and better technique
- There needs to be more professionalism introduced to the world of sports in India

CHAPTER 6

# INDIA'S VERY OWN FAIRY TALE

---

*"Call it the Big Bang of NBA fandom in China. Chinese basket-
ball fans began watching NBA games in 1987, the year in which
China Central Television (CCTV) began broadcasting NBA
games. Megastars such as Michael Jordan and Magic Johnson
instantly became household names. Then along came more
transformational American talents like Kobe Bryant, LeBron
James and Stephen Curry. Yao Ming, however, always has a
special place in Chinese fans' hearts. The 7-foot-6 center from
Shanghai isn't flashy. Unlike Allen Iverson, Yao's image is so clean
that it borders on boring. The color of Yao's Reebok sneakers is
so dull that for many years in China it lagged far behind Nike's
glamour shoes. He's too tall — basically no Chinese person can
relate to or emulate his playing style. Generation after generation, Chinese teenagers have worn baggy pants like Iverson or
Under Armour sneakers like Curry, mimicking the look and*

*moves of their idols. And they simply don't practice Yao's post*
*moves. But Yao is one of us. His experience is our experience;*
*his time is our time,"*

Santiago Muñez grew up in extreme poverty in Mexico. His
mother walked out on his family from as early as he can
remember and everything in his life just seemed to be stack-
ing up against him. His only escape was football - barefoot
on sandy and rocky dirt roads with crates as goals. It was all
he had to get away and stop thinking about his horrible life.
His father had been toiling away in construction during the
day and cleaning up a brothel at night to support his family
in hopes of saving up, to one day, be able to take his family to
America. One day Santi was woken up by his dad frantically
telling him to hurry. Santi grabbed a t-shirt and the only thing
that mattered to him - his football - before running out. He
jumped into a van with his family and a few other people
from the neighbourhood that had mustered up the courage
and money to try and cross the border to the greener side
and dreamland; otherwise known as the United States of
America. They made their way through the fence, avoiding
border patrol and successfully making it to Los Angeles. Cut
forward 10 years. Shaved head, 16 years old, roughly 6 foot tall,
Santi works as a gardener during the day and works a night
shift at an Asian restaurant in the city. He still plays football

and dreams of making it big. His dad, a man who has never had life help him out shuts him down and tells him to be realistic. One day, when Santi is playing for a local Sunday league team the ball goes out of play. A man in his mid 50's watching the scramble and mess of an under 8 game, turns to kick the ball back to the players, keeping an eye on the game for a split second. In that time, Santi gets the ball around the centre circle, spins past one player before playing a one-two with a teammate. He continues his run and flicks the ball up to himself before jumping and sending the ball flying past the keeper and into the back of the net. The man was pretty impressed. He continued watching before dissecting his technique whilst talking to Santi's coach.

"He doesn't look right. His balance is all wrong. Doesn't look up enough. Doesn't lift his legs high enough."

"That's what all the other teams think…" and, "then that happens," as Santi nutmegs a player before coolly slotting past the keeper.

The man stood, stunned.

A few months later, thanks to this very man, after a trial that didn't start out all that well, Santiago officially became a Newcastle United Football Club player. He had risen from literally nothing, to become a Premier League player.

This is the story of Goal! The Dream Begins. Santiago Muñez was the definition of a rags to riches story in one of the best sport movies (in my humble opinion at least). The story inspired a whole generation of kids that their dreams could come true.

Kids in England dream of bending it like David Beckham, kids in Portugal try to emulate Cristiano Ronaldo and kids in Argentina pray to be the next Messi. India needs its own Santiago Muñez. There needs to be a success story to push Indians towards playing football, there has to be a success story for India to buy into football. As I mentioned before, the perception of football is just a "game", where cricket can be a career if you're good enough. It is hard to look at football as a real option when not a single person from a country with a population that represents more than one sixth of the world has been able to make it. Yes, there are professional Indian players that earn a lot of money to do what they love, and yes there are a few Indian players plying their trades in Europe (be it at lowly clubs) but Indian football doesn't have a poster boy. There was recently a movie released on Mahindra Singh Dhoni, ex-captain of India's cricket team, that tells the story of his rise to fame. There is no such story in Indian football though. Sunil Chhetri and Bhaichung Bhutia are India's two highest goal scorers of all time and more importantly the two biggest names in Indian football. Bhaichung Bhutia became the first Indian to sign a contract with a European side in 1999 when he signed for Bury FC, a third division English club at the time. He spent three years there before returning to India in 2002. Sunil Chhetri was being touted as India's best ever football player. He had a year-long spell at Kansas City Wizards in 2010 which included an appearance against Manchester United in a friendly but no official appearances. He was then supposed to make his big break when he signed for Sporting Lisbon in 2012 but only ended up making 3 appearances for the reserves side that season before returning to India just a year later.

These are the two success stories of Indian football so far. The problem is that, while these two enjoyed a lot of success in their domestic careers, their careers abroad weren't as successful. Very, very few people outside of India would have heard of them and most people in India would struggle to name them if they saw them crossing the street. Even though they are supposed to be the two biggest names in the sport, they don't really have a celebrity status that is in anyway comparable to that of a cricketing star or a Bollywood actor.

Its the chicken and the egg story, really. What has to come first, the success story or the development of the game?

The success story? But, how can there be success if the sport isn't developed yet?

Okay, then the development of the game. But, how can the game develop if there is no reference story to look at and say, "oh yeah, it is possible"?

The truth is, that there is no definitive answer. The two have got to go hand-in-hand but eventually one has to happen first. One of the main goals of a project like the ISL, is to bring in some household names in football to inspire the new generation and show them what footballers can do and to show them that football really can get you somewhere in life.

In the movie Million Dollar Arm, before Rinku and Dinesh jet off to the US their parents are worried. How will they be able to cope? What is this man really selling us? Can we trust them? Baseball represents uncharted territory for Indians, the same way that football does.

India needs its own Dong Fangzhou, the first Chinese man to really sign a high-profile deal. There were others before him who had played in Europe but no one had played for a club as big as Manchester United.

### SATNAM SINGH:

The world of sports is without a doubt one of the most lucrative sectors in the world nowadays. While football definitely leads the march, perhaps it could learn a thing or two from some other sports, like basketball. In 2010, the National Basketball Association, the governing body of basketball in the US, hired Troy Justice as the Director of Basketball Operations in India in hopes of developing the sport in the Indian subcontinent. The NBA commissioner, Adam Silver, described India as a country where "the potential impact is beyond description". After, Yao Ming's success led to the development of basketball in China, the NBA was hoping to follow the same path and unearth some talent in India to unlock the door to a new talent market. "It really takes only one player from that country, to in essence, turn that switch. Yao Ming is the easiest example. When he came into the NBA, everything changed." Troy Justice set out on a mission to find basketball's poster child in India.

American entertainment giants, Netflix recently released a movie called "One in a Billion" covering the story of Satnam Singh - the first Indian to ever be drafted to the NBA.

It all started in Ballo Ke, a town in the north of India with a population of 800, where Satnam Singh lived with his family. Satnam was a giant, standing at 5 foot 9 before he even turned 10. A friend of his dad's convinced him to make Satnam start playing basketball, on the sole premise that "tall people are good at basketball". A few months later, Satnam went to Ludhiana to try out for a basketball academy after seeing an ad in a newspaper inviting all people over 6 foot to try out. Satnam started playing basketball without knowing how to hold a ball, he couldn't even differentiate between a volleyball and a basketball. In 2010, Troy Justice landed in India to look for his poster boy. When he asked where to find the most talented basketball players in the country he was directed to Ludhiana. Troy went straight there and the first thing he saw was a 14 year old Satnam Singh. With the help of IMG and Reliance, the NBA wanted to create opportunities in basketball in India and part of the agreement was to provide 8 scholarships to the world-famous IMG Academy in Bradenton, Florida. Satnam was amongst the chosen eight and flew 8000 miles across the world to begin a new life. The adjustment period was hard, but Satnam was happy to work knowing that if he could make something of himself he could, one day, support his entire family. Fast forward a couple years and the India basketball player had to start thinking about his next steps. All the top colleges in the country wanted to know about Satnam Singh but, because of his lack of English skills Satnam was forced to go back a grade and was therefore deemed ineligible for college by the NCAA. His saving grace was that he was eligible for the 2015 NBA Draft, however, because NBA laws stipulate that you must be five years removed from the start of the high school class and as a fifth-year senior he met this requirement. The big problem was whether Satnam was ready for the "big-time" yet, and most of the people around him didn't think he was.

"… and with the 52nd pick of the 2015 NBA Draft, the Dallas

Mavericks select Satnam Singh from Ball Ke, India"

These are the words that marked the turning point for Indian basketball. It now had its first ever player in the NBA. A true rags to riches story, where a boy who had never really even gone to school, because he had to spend his days working in the fields with his dad, made it to the NBA. Satnam has yet to make an appearance in the NBA, but started a movement in basketball in India and his true impact is yet to be seen. Football, too, has had a couple close calls but it hasn't come to the tipping point yet. And this leads me to my story.

I remember when I first travelled to Metz. I lived in Delhi at the time and had been working my ass off for the sport. My last six months in Delhi were some of the most intense days of my life. I was up everyday at 4 to train one-on-one with my coach, Yogesh. We would spend a couple hours on the pitch every morning doing intense drills, to get me sharp for my trial at the French club. After that, he would teach me tactics and help me with my mental preparation over breakfast. I would then go to school before my training sessions with my team or fitness trainer depending on the day. I wouldn't get home till 7 or 8 at night when I would have personal French lessons so that I wouldn't be completely lost when I got to Metz in the summer. I had to sacrifice a lot to prepare myself for the trial. I got to Metz feeling ready, though, I knew that I was as prepared as I was ever going to be. I went in confident, but had no real clue what to expect. My coaches were confident I could assure my spot at the club having previously spoken to some of the staff over in Metz as well as seeing a couple training sessions. But, I had no clue. I remember my first proper training session and specifically the scrimmage at the end of it. I was put in at right-back for the red team. The ball came to my feet straight from the kick-off, I brought it under control and looked up - BOOM. Before I knew it there was a man in my face and the ball was gone. I was frazzled and lost, I was used to being the best player on the pitch but I had barely even touched the ball and I was already a laughing stock. Fuck it, I thought. It was a one-off let's keep going. The opposite side's left winger picked up the ball deep in his own half and set off dribbling towards me. I saw a glimpse in his eye, he thought it would be a breeze in the park to go past me. He wasn't even a little intimidated, and nor should he have been... Before I could even react he knocked the ball to my left and ran around me to pick the ball up on the other side. I sat down in the changing room after, dead and embarrassed. I didn't understand a word that was being said, and really did not want to be there. A couple of the other players noticed this. They came over and patted me on the back, trying to convey a message in their frankly shit English. I was having none of it though, how could I be the one that everyone has pity for? I'm used to being the one that's giving everyone else nightmares! At least that's how it had been until then. Admittedly, that was one of my low points. It was a real shock. I never knew what it felt like to play that badly, but I had my ass handed to me that day and that's putting it nicely.

It took me a couple of days, but eventually I started to fit in and get my own back. I wasn't the laughing stock of the team anymore, they accepted me.

On the last day of my trial I remember packing up my things, itching to get home but more importantly shitting myself at the prospect of the final meeting with the Director of Youth Formation as well as the Under 17 Coach.

*"Shiv, you started off pretty badly. You seemed a little lost, very honestly and we were worried about you at the start. We weren't sure how you would cope with things, especially after the first training where you were à la ramasse (this directly translate to you were picking up the trash, or you were completely lost)...*

***FUCK. I HAD BLOWN IT. MY ONE BIG OPPORTUNITY AND I HAD BLOWN IT.***

*"But, you proved that you are both, mentally strong and a very good football player. We would love to have you at FC Metz. Go home, speak to your parents and let us know. We will be in touch about all the specifics.*

***Holy shit. Is he serious or is he just messing with me right now?***

I was absolutely ecstatic. This was insane, this was what I had been dreaming about since I was a kid.

To be quite honest, though, it wasn't until a couple months into my time as a Metz player that I realised just how big of a deal it was for me to be there. I remember waking up one morning, it was late November in 2012 an absolutely freezing already in the north of France. After hitting snooze 5 or 6 times, I finally dragged myself out of bed when my roommate was sick of hearing my alarm go off. I grabbed my phone and saw:

"423 Friend Requests, 284 Facebook Messages, 72 Messages, 146 WhatsApp Notifications, and 23 Missed Calls"

It was barely six in the morning and I was struggling to keep my eyes open, so it took me a second to read what it said. "Fucking hell, since when am I this popular," I thought. I'm usually a light sleeper but I didn't even hear my phone vibrate once, where did all these messages even come from. I scrolled through the messages and amongst the thousands of messages, every so often I saw a name that I recognised pop up. The vast majority though were alien to me, I had never heard of these people. Then, when I started to read what the messages said it became clear to me what had happened.

*The renowned academy in France is set to rope in two Delhi-based boys for a full-time training cum educational stint...*

In a period that has seen many youngsters being offered trials at foreign clubs, French club FC Metz has identified two Delhi-based youngsters to undergo a full-time training stint with the club.

The youngsters, Manas Kaalra and Shiv Jhangiani, underwent trials with the French club via Edukick Sports, a company started by Eric Benny, a former manager of the Indian national team. Benny and former US All Ivy League player, Yogesh Maurya oversaw the training of the Delhi boys for 3 years before offering them the chance to train at the FC Metz academy that has produced the likes of Robert Pires, Papiss Cisse, Emmanuel Adebayor and Louis Saha.

Shiv Jhangiani, who has already impressed Metz officials after his performances against the Luxembourg National team said, "In the three months that I have been here, I already feel part of the club. I stay with the other Academy players, train with them and go to school with them. I was lucky enough to train under Eric and Yogesh. They prepared me both on and off the field and the period of intense training proved invaluable in getting selected."

Manas Kaalra expressed his enthusiasm after knowing that he had been chosen for this unique opportunity. "Being at Metz is a dream come true for me. Being a professional footballer is something that I have strived for. I need to thank my coach Eric for developing me and helping me pursue my dream. He is more of a friend and mentor than a coach. I hope to make the best *of this opportunity and continue my development as a player so that I can compete with the best in the world," said Kaalra.*

*Eric Benny feels FC Metz's visits to India has helped them gauge the level of Indian football and pledged further contribution to help it reach the highest level.*

This article had been published on Goal.com, one of the most widely known football websites in the world, as well as a handful of Indian newspapers. I thought back and remember speaking to a few journalists in the weeks leading up to this. I remember being excited during the interviews to get some media coverage back home and told a few of my friends to keep their eyes open, but I never expected this big of a reaction. It was insane. I was definitely hoping, and expecting to some extent, to get a few messages and get a quick second of fame but I never thought it would be this big. Once I went through a bunch of the messages and read them properly, I realised not only how lucky I was to be where I was but also how important it was for me to do well. I wasn't just representing myself, or my family, I was representing India. I was representing 1.3 billion people. I was one of the first two Indian youth players to be training at a professional European club.

Hundreds of thousands of kids back home dreamed of playing football day-in-day-out at a club in Europe, but I was the one that was given that opportunity.

It was a pretty big fucking deal.

I was only a 15 year old kid, but I felt the pressure and felt the responsibility. I felt the weight on my shoulders. This definitely raised expectations, but I liked that. It only made me want to go further, work harder and succeed more.

Unfortunately, things never quite panned out the way I had envisioned and hoped but I haven't lost a speck of my love for football. If an article about a couple teenagers training at a European club with a fairly low profile, relatively speaking, could have such a reaction imagine how India would react to the news of Manchester United signing an Indian. The country would go mental!

Indian football is a sitting on the edge right now and is quickly approaching the tipping point.

**TAKEAWAY:**

- With no precedent for success on the international level for India in football, we need a flag bearer at the top level.
- One break is all it is going to take to push India over the edge.
- The financial opportunities for the first European club to play an Indian are endless.

# CONCLUSION

———

Indian football is showing signs of promise. The game of football is globalised, but India represents a rarity in this world - an untapped market. India is uncharted territory and the opportunities that exist are endless. With talent to be found as well as money to be made, it is attractive from all standpoints. India is at a stage where it needs the right investors to come in and take the sport to the next level. Things are definitely moving in the right direction, and the right amount of money along with the right ideas will propel India to the top.

**Let's take a look at what could be to come for India if things pan out well.**

## JUNE 2038

The feeling of excitement and expectation are looming in Indian air as we are gearing up for the start of the first ever FIFA World Cup to be held in India. The opening game will take place at the newly renovated Salt Lake Stadium in Kolkata between England and hosts, India. The inventors of the game against the up and coming team. Hopes are high in India and the people are expecting big things in this tournament from the home country despite it only being their second ever appearance at a FIFA World Cup. We are here today with the man who started the footballing revolution in India; the man who is being dubbed the "Godfather of Indian Football", Shiv Jhangiani.

Shiv, pleasure to have you here today. Could you have ever seen this day coming?

*Honestly, yes. I know it's hard to believe but I always knew this day would never be too far. If I didn't believe in it, I would have never taken on the role of India's Head of Football Development. We have honestly come a long, long way but this is only the start - it is not the finish.*

Let's go all the way back to the start. What made you want to get involved in developing football in India?

*As far back as I can remember, football has been more than just a part of my life - it has been my life. Growing up I moved around a lot, living in 7 different countries before even getting to college. In each of these countries, football was a lot, lot more than just a sport. It was a way of life. This was true for every country except for two: the US and India. It was in Greece that I began to think that I could really make something of myself through the sport. I was playing for a club over there in organised leagues from the Under 5 category all the way through to the Under 12 category. Then, I moved to India and there was nothing. The only football I was playing was during the lunch break at school with some friends and then for my school team. But, there were no real opportunities. No clubs like in Greece. No leagues. Nothing really. I got very lucky though. I was in the right place at the right time and was lucky enough to meet the right people. Some of the very few people that were involved in football in India at the time. This led to a number of opportunities and eventually led to me playing FC Metz's youth teams. My time at Metz was incredible. I realised just how lucky I was to be there and realised the responsibility and the weight that was on my shoulders. Unfortunately, the program went downhill and things for me went the same way. A couple major injuries to my knee ruled me out for 2 years between the ages of 16 and 18, 2 of the most important formative years in a footballer's career. The odds were already against me going pro because of the fact that my time in India saw my progression as a footballer regress rather than move forward. But then, after the injuries, things just didn't work out. I was adamant that football had to be where I ended up and would not let that go. I knew that there were a lot of different avenues I could go down to get back into the sport. Despite having only spent 3 years in India, I have always grown up and felt Indian, so to see that my home country had no real presence in football was upsetting to me. I knew that this was what I wanted to do, make India a world-footballing power.*

How did you first get involved, then?

*Obviously I wasn't given the Head of Development job till further down the line. It started with a couple projects that I invested in with some partners. Then we looked to approach different European clubs to get them involved in India. At that stage a lot of clubs supposedly had a presence in India but the problem was that it was indirect. The clubs weren't sending their own people and weren't really as involved as they needed to be to succeed in India. One team signed me on as their Head of Development in India. I was the man charged with leading the club's movement in India. And this is where things really kicked off because I was exposed to a lot and was forced to learn on the job. I was meeting with officials from the governing body, understanding the details of the field and really understanding what needed to happen.*

You have been drawn in the group of death featuring giants Brazil and England along with dark horses of the tournament, the United States. What are your expectations of India at this World Cup?

*Well just like any other Indian I am hoping for the best. We ⋅have to be realistic, and not put too much pressure on the lads, though. We are very well prepared going into the tournament, the conditions will be tough for other teams but we know exactly what to expect. We have to be realistic in terms of how far we can go, but I see no reason why we can't make it out of the group. It is true that we have been drawn a tough group but at the end of the day it is the World Cup. We were never going to get an easy draw. I am happy that we've got the teams we have in our group. The boys probably wouldn't have needed any extra motivation but if they ever did, facing the likes of Brazil and England is enough to make you drool. Just having India at a World Cup is a dream that very few people thought they would see in their lifetime when I was younger.*

You mentioned that not a lot of people expected this. But, where did you expectations come from?

*Well football has been at the centre of my life ever since I can remember. Unfortunately, things never quite worked out as a player for me but I didn't let my dreams die with my playing career. I was determined to be the man to change the landscape of Indian football. My time at FC Metz was always going to be valuable to me in terms of understanding the footballing world and establishing contacts in the game. The first step was bringing organisation to Indian football. When I was brought in, there was just no clear vision of what needed to be done. We had to set out a step-by-step plan, detailing every little thing. Just like anything in life, you can never be too close minded and we have had to adjust to reality along the way so have not stuck to the plan completely. We were forced to think on our feet and get ourselves out of some sticky situations.*

Can you tell us, concretely, how did you bring football in India to the stage it is at today?

*Well we knew that bringing in experts was always going to be key. The first thing to do was to set an identity for Indian football, this could not be set in stone though as we didn't really have much of an idea of what Indian football was at that stage. So, we tried to set things out the way we wanted them to be but had to be open-minded to things changing. Today, the quick passing and high pressing style of football that is played by the national team is no mere coincidence. Yes, it can only work if you have the right profile of players but we knew what the average Indian player would be like a long time ago.*

*The first three major programs that I rolled out were the Pre-Youth Program, the Infrastructure Development and the coaching courses. These are the three pillars of the sport in India today, in my eyes. Developing a passion and understanding of the game from ages as young as 2 was key. You cannot start playing football at the age of 7 or 8, we had to engrain football into our culture because it is between the ages of 2 and 6 that kids develop their coordination skills. Ball manipulation is one of the most important aspects and we were falling far behind our counterparts across the world just because kids wouldn't start playing the game till later. Developing infrastructure was another integral part of the plan. We had to build pitches across the country for kids to be able to play. Initially, it wasn't about having state of the art training facilities or the biggest stadiums in the world. It was just about creating playing surfaces so that there were pitches available to everyone. The weather conditions in India made this a tough prospect, as enduring the months of monsoon was always tough. The Coaching Courses was the third and final piece to the jigsaw puzzle at the start. When Germany had to reinvent itself, it was forced to increase the number of coaches. In India, we had very few coaches but a lot of people interested in the sport and teaching it. The expertise of European clubs like FC Metz was needed in training coaches and setting up courses like the ones we held. It was very important to hold separate courses for different types of coaches, for example a first team coach would struggle to effectively coach an Under 5 team because the skill set of the players is completely different.*

Apart from the three programs you mentioned, are there any other specific changes or programs you feel had a big impact?

Changing the league system in India was massive. You look at what the I-League and ISL were, compared to the league we have today. We tried to bring together the best of both worlds whilst adapting it to India. Having two different competitions made no sense and was never going to help Indian football. The 3-month version of the ISL was fairly successful but drawing out the same plan over a longer period of time wasn't going to be that simple. There had to be a proper league set up. Having said that, we couldn't just put in a traditional league that you would see in England or Germany, we had to recognise the success of the ISL and even the IPL, amongst fans in India.

It was important to be clear that Indian talent had to be a priority for everyone involved in the league. If we don't promote our own, who will? We had to make sure that Indian players were getting playing time and getting the exposure they needed to be able to develop.

The youth leagues are another key part. Not only does it set up a funnel of talent for each of the professional teams, it also sets up a platform for the young players to showcase their talent on and potentially get signed by foreign teams. Signing partnerships with some of the biggest teams in Europe to bring in their personnel to help reshape the clubs over here was massive. Their know-how and expertise couldn't be reformulated overnight.

In a country as big as India, how did you know where to start?

*Well there were only pockets of India, at that time, where football was really a part of the culture. We used to call these the "Pockets of Promise". We had to start somewhere and there could be no wrong answer, the question was where would our plans have the biggest impact in the shortest amount of time though as this would be our platform to launch everything. Cricket is, and was, the king sport in India, we would have been fools to try and take on cricket. It would be like showing up to a gun-fight with a knife! What we had to do was tap into the underlying football culture, which was a lot more prominent in these "Pockets of Promise". Kolkata, Goa and then the states in the northeast made up these areas.*

An essential part of the programs was the partners you had. How did you manage to attract such prominent partners and sponsors when there was barely any presence of Indian football?

*Yes of course. Each one of the partners and sponsors has been an integral part of the journey of Indian football. Without them I am certain that we would not be here today anticipating the start of a FIFA World Cup in India. I was just going around pitching the opportunity to anyone that was kind enough to listen at the start to be honest. Beggars can't be choosers and opportunities were certainly few and far between at the start. I felt like I had a compelling case and really believed in what I was pitching, I think this helped. You must remember that*

*India's economy was absolutely booming and the potential for development was endless. We had nothing to lose because the current state of football in India was quite simply abysmal. Once we got the first few on board we knew that the others would regret turning down the opportunity and would be lining up to get involved in any way possible later down the line. It took a lot of convincing but I put my neck on the line to close the first few deals, I honestly believed from the very beginning that the Indian market presented the world of football with an immense opportunity. The first few clubs to get involved could be assured to have a pipeline of talented players coming through for many, many years to come.*

Many have claimed that Manchester United's pre season tour of India in 2020 was a turning point. What are your thoughts on this?

*They were definitely important in showing the Indian people what could come if we were to develop football in our country. But, I think it had an even bigger influence on the corporates. We found it tough to convince companies in India to sponsor these tours at the start. In fact, Manchester United were the first team to tour India and it wasn't till two weeks before they arrived that we secured the sponsorship fee. This tour was a proof of concept, a proof of a deep rooted love of the beautiful game in India. Once other clubs started to come and we held tournaments, things really began to tick. We were able to start attracting a lot of talent to the domestic leagues and this raised the standard of Indian football. Having some of the biggest names in world football playing in India was also big because it opened the eyes of the new generation to the glamorous world of football. I myself grew up as a Manchester United fan and seeing the Salt Lake Stadium in a sea of red really brought tears to my eyes.*

What were some of the biggest challenges you faced initially?

*Well, one of the biggest problems at the time with Indian football was that there were businessmen and politicians at the head of the football governing body. They were setting unrealistic goals and expectations that were never going to be met. There were just too many people involved that were looking for a short term pay off, they couldn't really care less about developing football. When I came in, I had to sit down and tell them to their face what too many people were afraid to say, "we need to start from scratch."*

What were some of the goals that you set out for yourself at the start then?

*If you look at the history of football, teams don't just qualify for World Cup's by luck or by chance. There is a very long, detailed process that has qualifying for a World Cup at the end. I was being asked for a timeline constantly, but had to keep pleading with them to not make it a ticking time bomb. It was tough because I myself didn't have a definitive time line set out. I just knew that there were checkpoints we had to reach and there were obviously rough estimates for when these would happen, and if we didn't reach them around that time we knew something was going wrong.*

Were there any major setbacks along your journey?

*Of course, and there are always going to be. This is what I have my board to thank for. They stuck with me and kept believing in me in moments of difficulty. We had hoped to reach the World Cup in 2034 but missed out by the skin of our teeth, it was very disappointing but now I wouldn't have it any other way. It's almost fitting that our debut be at home.*

Finally, if there is one point in time that you can pick as the major turning point for football in India what would it be?

*Football is a team sport and developing it as such was one of the main ideologies behind the whole movement. There are a lot of key dates along the way but, if I had to pick one moment it would have to be have to be the day we were awarded the World Cup. The pinnacle of world football, the most watched live event known to man and the tournament to crown the champions of the world's most popular sport. It just does not get any bigger than that. India at the centre stage of the world.*

*And, it meant a lot more than just hosting the tournament to us. It meant playing in the World Cup. If you ask any football fan in the world what their dream is, I can guarantee you that each and every one of them would say to captain their team to a World Cup Finals. and Mr. Jay Singh is the luckiest man in India, the opportunity to lead out not just 10 men but a whole nation to the World Cup Finals, well it truly is the stuff of dreams. Tomorrow, will go down in the history of India right alongside August the 15th of 1947 - the day of our independence and I don't mean that as a joke.*

Mr. Jhangiani, thank you very much for your time. We know you won't be getting much sleep and nor will the billion other fans tonight in anticipation of what is being called "the second birth of India".

Till tomorrow and to end this, on your, very appropriate, favourite phrase in football commentary: **you couldn't write a script like this.**

Printed in Great Britain
by Amazon